CAMBRIDGE LIBRARY COLLECTION

Books of enduring scholarly value

History

The books reissued in this series include accounts of historical events and movements by eye-witnesses and contemporaries, as well as landmark studies that assembled significant source materials or developed new historiographical methods. The series includes work in social, political and military history on a wide range of periods and regions, giving modern scholars ready access to influential publications of the past.

With Thackeray in America

The British painter Eyre Crowe, through words and illustrations, chronicled his six-month American tour with William Makepeace Thackeray. Crowe accompanied Thackeray in the unfamiliar role of his secretary during Thackeray's U.S. lecture circuit in 1852–3, and his illustrated account was published in 1893 – thirty years after the writer's death – under the title, With Thackeray In America. Crowe relates that the renowned writer asked him to accompany him for the simple reason that 'Six months tumbling about the world will do you no harm.' A lasting and memorable partnership was formed, and the details of the adventure were preserved in Crowe's humorous running commentary as well as in his art.

Cambridge University Press has long been a pioneer in the reissuing of out-of-print titles from its own backlist, producing digital reprints of books that are still sought after by scholars and students but could not be reprinted economically using traditional technology. The Cambridge Library Collection extends this activity to a wider range of books which are still of importance to researchers and professionals, either for the source material they contain, or as landmarks in the history of their academic discipline.

Drawing from the world-renowned collections in the Cambridge University Library, and guided by the advice of experts in each subject area, Cambridge University Press is using state-of-the-art scanning machines in its own Printing House to capture the content of each book selected for inclusion. The files are processed to give a consistently clear, crisp image, and the books finished to the high quality standard for which the Press is recognised around the world. The latest print-on-demand technology ensures that the books will remain available indefinitely, and that orders for single or multiple copies can quickly be supplied.

The Cambridge Library Collection will bring back to life books of enduring scholarly value (including out-of-copyright works originally issued by other publishers) across a wide range of disciplines in the humanities and social sciences and in science and technology.

With Thackeray
in America

EYRE CROWE

CAMBRIDGE
UNIVERSITY PRESS

CAMBRIDGE UNIVERSITY PRESS

Cambridge, New York, Melbourne, Madrid, Cape Town, Singapore,
São Paolo, Delhi, Dubai, Tokyo

Published in the United States of America by Cambridge University Press, New York

www.cambridge.org
Information on this title: www.cambridge.org/9781108002998

© in this compilation Cambridge University Press 2009

This edition first published 1893
This digitally printed version 2009

ISBN 978-1-108-00299-8 Paperback

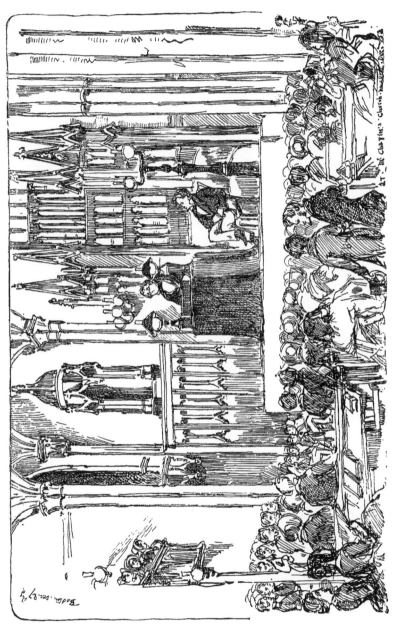

THACKERAY LECTURING AT NEW YORK

WITH THACKERAY

IN AMERICA

BY

EYRE CROWE, A.R.A.

ILLUSTRATED

NEW YORK
CHARLES SCRIBNER'S SONS
1893

THIS BOOK

DUE TO SIX MONTHS' CONSTANT TRAVEL WITH

HER FATHER

IS WITH HER KIND PERMISSION DEDICATED TO

MRS. RICHMOND RITCHIE

AS A TRIBUTE OF ADMIRATION FOR HER INHERITED

LITERARY GIFTS AND FOR THE SAKE OF

A LIFE-LONG FRIENDSHIP

EYRE CROWE

London
20th February 1893

PREFACE

ALL readers of Thackeray know his delightful
imaginary conversation-verses between " The Pen and
the Album," written before his travels in the United
States, and the concluding lines :—

> " Stranger ! I never writ a flattery,
> Nor sign'd the page that register'd a lie."

" The faithful old Gold Pen," to which he assigns
these two noble qualifications of unswerving truthful-
ness, and which he then adds had served him already
for three long years in making his sketches, was part of
his equipment of materials taken to the States.   When
it was not in his own grasp he allowed me to take
it up for my sketching lucubrations, which were for
the most part executed with its wondrously flexible
and seemingly indestructible nib.   He was so far
pleased with my efforts that, not content with show-
ing them to our American friends, who also nodded
approvingly over their sometimes grotesque yet faithful renderings of every-day scenes as they struck a

newcomer's fancy, he urged me to make a selection
from them, and to forward them to London for publication in an illustrated periodical. Whether they ever
reached their destination I forgot to ascertain on my
return. This neglect on my part I now lament, as
among the drawings was one of the Washington
House of Representatives, with a portrayal of the
different members sitting at their semi-circularly-
placed desks, fronting the Speaker's Chair, over which
soared majestically the American eagle. This loss
must be my apology for omitting from this collection
any representation of the holders of the great political helm of the States. Perhaps the chance owner
may hereafter let me know of its whereabouts, and
in case of future editions, if any, kindly allow me to
repair the gap.

Whilst contrasting the scenes delineated forty
years ago with subsequent accounts which have
reached us in numberless books of travel, not to
mention the useful successive "Appleton Guide"
editions, I have been struck with the appositeness
of Carlyle's epithet applied to progressive Columbia,
as "the never-resting locomotive country." What
was then fact may now seem to border on fiction.
But, for my own part, I trust that this may be accepted as a record of actual life imbued with the
subtle spirit of truth flowing from "the faithful old

Gold Pen," and not belying the honest character ascribed to it by the owner.

I may take this opportunity of here thanking my kind friend Mr. Wemyss Reid, who encouraged me to publish these sketches and their accompanying text.

The *Illustrated London News* printed a very few of the illustrations in the old familiar wood-cut manner, now superseded for the most part by other facsimile processes, justifying their re-insertion here. *Household Words* also published my account of the Virginian slave sale, which has now been amplified with incidents there omitted for the sake of brevity.

CONTENTS

CHAPTER I

CHAPTER II

CHAPTER III

CHAPTER IV

CHAPTER V

LIST OF ILLUSTRATIONS

WITH THACKERAY
IN AMERICA

THE EMBLEM OF OFFICE

WITH THACKERAY IN AMERICA

CHAPTER I

"Esmond"—Lectures at Liverpool and Manchester—Savile Morton—Voyage across the Atlantic—Boston—Custom House—Shandry-dan—Tremont—A Rapid Repast—Bunker's Hill—MM. Prescott and Ticknor—In the Cars—"Thackeray's Works"—Arrival in New York—Mr. Bancroft—Spirit-Rapping—The Rev. Theodore Parker and Horace Greeley.

"SIX months' tumbling about the world will do you no harm," was the inducing phrase which Thackeray used when he kindly asked me to accompany him as his factotum and amanuensis on his forthcoming journeyings in the United States. When he noticed my hesitation as to acceptance of the post, arising in a great measure from my doubts as to my having

the proper capacity—or " spryness," as he expressed it
—for organising and arranging the business part of
the lecturing, he pointed out that another half-year
would elapse before his departure, and that I could try
my 'prentice-hand, first, during these months, in the
same capacity. 'Twas thus I found myself installed
in doing secretarial work at his pleasant Kensingtonian
home in Young Street. The emblem of office, a
knowing-looking green dispatch-box, of which the
outer leather case bore many traces of long and honour-
able use in Continental travel, was presented to me by
the owner, then possessor of a more splendid desk. I
retain it now—not only as a valued memento and gift
of the owner, but as reminding me of the many
pleasant epistolary, documentary, and sketching
fragments it contained during my subsequent stay
in America. A selection of these sketches has been
made, upon which the following text may be taken
as merely a running commentary.

Two scraps of paper lying for two-score years dormant in this receptacle, in pocket-books, will serve to
show the sort of mingled preoccupations engaging the
author at that time, and will illustrate the easy
duties involved in secretaryship. The first is a
memorandum directing me to make inquiries at the
British Museum.

When my new indoctrination as amanuensis

began, the first portion of " Esmond " was completed, written upon small slips of note-paper kept in the firm grip of an elastic band. They were not written, as was the case with the calligraphy of his great proto-type the novel-writer Balzac, in crabbed handwriting, bristling with after-thought emendations, but, on the contrary, in the beautiful penmanship so well known, and of which the annexed slip is another example,

and with scarcely any interpolations or marginal *repentirs*. The person who stated that all the writing of " Esmond " MS. was dictated was, therefore, to that extent inexact. The passage to which the note refers

is in the second book of "Esmond," and contained,
I think, in about the fifteenth chapter. I went to
the great and unique source of all English trustworthy
information, the British Museum, and I asked for the
Gazettes as printed in 1708 by the great Jacob
Tonson, in Gray's Inn Gate, and I ferreted out the
items to be incorporated in the narrative. But this
last became so complex, as the author went on with
his story, that he had to trust not alone to vicarious
excerpts, but used to charter a cab and to come along
with me to the British Museum. An appeal to an
obliging attendant brought us through the non-public
portion of the Library, where, I remember, on his
touching a hidden spring in what seemed to be
beautifully bound folios, but which were in reality
only the sham backs of these, a door flew open, and
we were ' in the presence of Sir Antonio Panizzi,
whose life Mr. Fagan has so pleasantly unfolded in
after-years. He readily granted permission to write
in one of the secluded galleries, at a table placed in
the midst of the volumes to be consulted. I sat down
and wrote to dictation the scathing sentences about
the great Marlborough, the denouncing of Cadogan,
etc., etc. As a curious instance of literary contagion,
it may be here stated that I got quite bitten with the
expressed anger at their misdeeds against General
Webb, Thackeray's kinsman and ancestor; and that I

then looked upon Secretary Cardonnel's conduct with perfect loathing. I was quite delighted to find his meannesses justly pilloried in " Esmond's " pages.

It was not without peculiar piquancy that this was done upon the site of old Montague House and its gardens, famous in those Queen Anne days; as " Prue," Steele's wife, exclaimed : " This is where you wretches go and fight duels." To save ears polite, the irascible expletive applied to Cardonnel, printed in full in the first edition, was mitigated to the more presentable " d——d " form in after-issues.

Equally complaisant were the secretary and com- mittee of the Athenæum Club, where the same method of dictation was pursued in one of the side rooms off the large library there. I do not recollect that these utterances, not at all delivered *sotto voce*, disturbed the equanimity of either Church, law, or science dignitaries frequenting that luxuriously seated library.

A red-letter day was Saturday, May 28th, when Thackeray was able to write the word " End," thus concluding the " History of Esmond." It was, I recollect, on a pleasant balmy day, and the work had proceeded in accordance with that atmosphere to its close. A friendly party had been invited to dinner, and he expressed a wish that I should join the circle. The temptation was great—with the prospect of drinking a bumper to success. My habiliments, however, were not of the festive, but of the workaday sort, and I could not readily get another suit; so I lost the chance of celebrating the event in proper trim.

The visit to America then came uppermost.

A week before this date, as may be seen from the following letter addressed by Thackeray to Mr. Felt, the formal proposal had reached London.

13, *Young Street, Kensington.*
May 21*st*, 1852.

SIR,—

His Excellency the American Minister [The Hon. Abbott Lawrence, Min. Plen.] has forwarded to me your kind letter and proposal, for which I return my best thanks to the directors of the Mercantile Library at New York.

My wish is to deliver in that city and elsewhere in the United States the six lectures [on the English humorous writers of Queen Anne's reign] that have been received with great favour in this country. I have no agent in America, and purposed to enter into no arrangements until I arrived myself at New York or Boston, and could determine personally what would be the best course to pursue.

If, as your kind letter suggests, arrangements could be made by which I could deliver my lectures in several cities of the Union, and proposals to that effect were made to me, I should very thankfully entertain them—premising always that no objection would be made to my giving lectures to other public societies, and at such charges as my friends at New York and elsewhere might think advisable.

MILLARD L. FELT, ESQ.,   Etc. Etc.
Corresponding Secretary, Mercantile Library.

This was the beginning of a somewhat lengthened correspondence. The Boston author and publisher Mr. Fields had already made suggestions as to lecturing there. Questions of priority soon cropped up, ultimately left for final solution till the arrival in the States.

The summer months glided by, chiefly employed in revising the " Esmond " proof-sheets, a slower process than is usually the case, owing to a comparatively small supply of the not-much-used type of the reign of Queen Anne, which was one of the features of the first edition.

A new club had at this time sprung into life, called by Thackeray the " Fielding," which met in Henrietta Street, Covent Garden. His contribution to its comfort was an illustrated screen, print-covered for the most part, but made more valuable by the addition of two of his own gold-pen-and-ink studies. The subjects were two street Arabs caught in the law's meshes. The first was in the grip of a Bow Street runner of Fielding's time; in the next a tattered son of St. Giles was being "run in" by the modern Bobby, who hauls him before the Beak, with a view to his improvement in a reformatory.

Mrs. Ritchie has, in her pleasant "Chapters from some Unwritten Memoirs," told her numerous readers of her father's genuine relish of Carlyle's "enchanting screen," to which he had also contributed. And, years ago, I recollect his amused scanning of the motley prints upon the *paravent* of the "Trafalgar" at Greenwich—before the advent of "souchet" and whitebait—to which he had invited us. But as the "Trafalgar" has closed its doors, so has the once hospitable Fielding Club—to which I recollect also being invited as a guest—made way for more modern brickwork. Many guests have vanished thence. I wonder where these pleasant screen-appurtenances have gone to?

I often have wished for the stenographic power, which enables many chroniclers to give the charm of the random talk of gifted men. Far pleasanter are these rapid utterances than the more poised sentences of public speaking. In this latter vein is on record the speech made at the "Freemasons' Tavern" this year by Thackeray as he presided at the Literary Fund Dinner.

At the end of September we went down to Liverpool, celebrating the inauguration of the lecturing tour by testing the famous "clear turtle" of the "Adelphi" there, ere we went into more homely quarters during our fortnight's stay. A veil is drawn here over this "memorial of gormandising," which, in truth, was sober enough.

The twin courses of lectures given in the two first

October weeks were thus dove-tailed as to time and delivery—

MANCHESTER		LIVERPOOL	
Tuesdays.	*Thursdays.*	*Wednesdays.*	*Fridays.*
28th Sept.	30th Sept.	29th Sept.	1st Oct.
5th Oct.	7th Oct.	6th Oct.	8th "
12th "	14th "	13th "	15th "

This arrangement necessitated see-sawing by train from one place to the other.

There was a curious contrast in the initial reception of the lectures in these Lancashire centres, the rooms of the Manchester Athenæum being well filled, but at the Liverpool Philharmonic Hall, on the contrary, the audience was so small as to call forth from one signing himself " Dickey Sam " (in the *Liverpool Mercury* of October 1st) the statement " that a more heart-depressing sight than that which presented itself to Mr. Thackeray, I think I have never witnessed, to hear the Fielding of the nineteenth century." The subsequent lectures, however, made amends; and the whole course, in both places, went off with great *éclat.*

At Liverpool cheery lodgings in Renshaw Street, over Parry's Library, were found for us; and free use was made of its stock of books—the Public Library, which only opened a few days after

we left, being then unavailable — Steele's Letters
and Bozzy's Life of Johnson coming in for re-
perusal as old friends and ever-fresh companions.
I only recollect that here Thackeray, in the interval of awaiting the lecture hour in the little side room
of the Philharmonic, either translated or amended
his version of Béranger's beautiful lines in "Ma
Vocation"—

> "Jeté sur cette boule,
> Laid, chétif, et souffrant," etc.

I forget whether, as first given in his Goldsmith
lecture, the lines were read in French or not.

During his stay at Liverpool occurred a tragical
event, which happened on the 4th, but which was
only reported the next day, the 5th of October. On
opening a paper Thackeray read a brief telegram
announcing that his friend Savile Morton, the Paris
correspondent of the *Daily News*, had been stabbed—
dying of his wounds—by a brother-journalist, seized
with a fit of frenzied rage against him. It caused a
great shock of surprise to us both, whose friend he
had been. Thackeray mournfully recapitulated his
many charming qualities; his artistic early education, merged, like his own, into more bread-winning
literature; and finally alluded to his many Bohemian
adventures, summing up his life as having been

"one scrape." His loss was much felt by the staff of the paper he had served so faithfully.

In lounging through the gay streets, thronged with an interesting population of seafarers and others, I recollect Thackeray's gaze being riveted for some time looking into a printshop at a likeness of another lost friend, late the chief magistrate of Liverpool, Edward Rushton. The print recalled old days of boon-companionship and Reform Club foregatherings; and so, with a regretful "How like it is!" we passed on. Unpleasant sensations, it is said, seldom come singly; so it turned out now. On seeking a resting-place for weary limbs, we turned into the literary institution called the Athenæum, where English and American newspapers were to be seen. He chanced upon an article in a New York sheet containing a bitter philippic upon no less a person than himself. It belonged to that now exploded form of bitter personality. It denounced as uncalled for his intended visit to the United States, as encouraging that already too numerous class of lecturers who first mulct the citizens of their dollars, and then return to their own country to lampoon them. It was felt at first as a decided damper. But further reflection made him think the onslaught harmless, and the sting in it only of the pin-prod order.

The latter half of October was spent in farewell visits to friends, Thackeray spending most of his time in London. His correspondence of this time is saddened by a dash of foreboding bodily ills— which, luckily, were not fulfilled.

On a fine autumnal day, the golden leafage in English pastures being at its best, we left London by train for Liverpool, the first stage of our journey to the States ; this was on the 29th of October.

About a hundred passengers, as an after-reference to the name-list showed us, were doing the same.

Thackeray had been invited, as well as myself, to take shelter on this last evening in the hospitable house of Mr. Ratcliffe, of the firm of Bailey Brothers, iron-masters ; and we drove to Clarence Terrace, which commands a fine view of the Mersey and its shipping. A friendly party met at dinner ; amongst the rest the Mayor of Liverpool, Mr. Thomas Littledale. The *pièce de résistance* at the banquet, in the shape of roast sucking-pig, was received with all the honours of loud laughter. The considerate hostess, knowing the Thackerayan fondness for that succulent joint, had prepared this surprise for him, and had donned it in its appetising crackle-coating. But, of course, the prospective sailors, as well as their brother-guests, felt that this was hardly the proper foundation

for meeting stoutly the heaving billows of the
morrow. Undaunted, however, by the somewhat
dubious results foreshadowed, full justice was done
to this part of the *menu*, breaking up the festivities,
in first-rate humour, late in the evening.

The next day, October 30th, we bade farewell to
our kind hosts, and before ten o'clock, the appointed
hour, we found ourselves, on a bright sunshiny morning, waiting for the tender at the end of the landing
stage. Whilst we were looking out for it, and mind-
ing that no traps were missing, a messenger suddenly
arrived with a large batch of correspondence and a
yet larger square brown-paper parcel. On opening
the latter Thackeray found therein several copies of
" Esmond," in three volumes, of which this instalment,
the first issued, reached him just in time before
starting. He turned over the uncut leaves, expressed
himself well pleased with this *finale* of lengthened
labour on his part, and thought the Smith and Elder
firm had well capped their acceleration of production
of the proof-sheets with this wind-up of their neat
binding ere he left the English shore.

The tender came alongside ; we embarked upon
it, and were soon clambering up the ladder swung
on the sides of the royal mail ship *Canada* (Captain
Lang), the gallant vessel moving along as we did so.
We felt, as most do on such occasions, that the ship

looked much smaller than our anticipations had led us
to expect, and was not such as to correspond in importance with the renowned personages in the world of

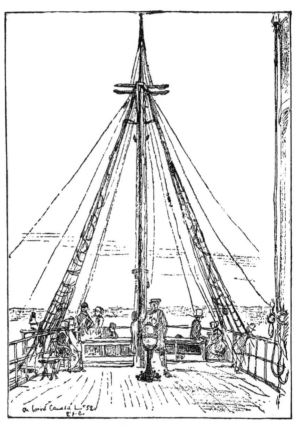

ON BOARD THE "CANADA"

literature now grouped together on board. Besides
Thackeray, there was Russell Lowell, fresh from
Italy. Coming up the companion ladder, I noticed a

burly form, in mustard-coloured inexpressibles, and a
wideawake hat crowning a swarthy face. This was
Arthur Hugh Clough, the poet and Oxford Don,
whose published Diary gives a pleasant account of
this voyage and of the people on board. I have preserved the sketch of a few of them as they clustered
round the binnacle. Towering above all in size,
you note, chatting, Titmarsh himself, with head and
travelling-cap above the line of the horizon.

I soon discovered that I did not belong to that
class of people who follow the advice of enterprising
encyclopædic dictionary publishers, to buy and read
their volumes through on a sea voyage, emerging
from their perusal at the end in the possession of a
portentous fund of knowledge. I preferred sketching
to reading. Here
are selected a few
of these jottings.

First notice,
Captain Lang, sex-
tant in hand, deter-
mining our where-
abouts at noon, if
the sun appeared
at that convenient
juncture. Also
his lieutenant

The Captain Taking an Observation

officer ditto

assisting him in this important operation. Next is a passenger, for whom his co-mates clubbed together to present him with a valuable razor and piece of soap on arrival, as he seemed utterly destitute of these two commodities. The sailors' dress and their well-knit forms always afford good lines, whether "heaving the log," as here seen, or giving a coat of paint to the masts or spar-gear.

When nearing Cape Race the vessel was brought-to, and the engines suddenly ceased to throb, the steamer balancing on a gentle swell. Conversations ceased; everybody watched to see what would be revealed by the deep-sea lead. (Brother land-lubbers, please pronounce "dipsey-lead" as you here gaze at its shape and its tell-tale indicator

A PASSENGER

of depth of the sea under you full many a
fathom.) 'Twas all right; we were in our proper
course; the lights ceased to twinkle; on the vessel
ploughed once more for Halifax. When that port

THE DEEP-SEA LEAD

was reached, I remained below, and thus missed
the chance of landing and seeing the place in
darkness. I afterwards heard that when refreshing
themselves at this nocturnal bar, by a sudden frolic
some passengers put up to mock auction the negro
attendant, who was run up to a tremendous price.
The freeman probably took it as a great compliment, and as an acknowledgment of his efficiency
in the serving line.

2

It was a delightful sensation to be steaming between the rocky reefs on entering the Boston harbour, after being pent up for so many days. Our captain donned his best suit, and appeared on deck silver trumpet in hand ; and after bumping against a pier, then backing once more, he sent out the hawser, which now bound us to the New England shore. We had, overhead, a most glorious sunset effect of cloudland, quite eclipsing the now already darkening outline of the distant town of Boston. Thackeray looked on, interested to watch the numerous forms of greeting of friends. As yet there were no visible signs of his visit being expected ; an absence of demonstrativeness quite at variance with former unburthening of welcome, as described by Dickens and others. The *facetiæ* perpetrated in the " American Notes " had damped the enthusiastic ardour of the Yankees, who now hung out no exuberant bunting. There seemed to be not even a solitary interviewing reporter to greet the lecturer as he stood, his small bag in hand, looking on at the bustling crowds. This was, however, only simulated reticence ; they soon showed abundant proofs of a hearty predisposition in his favour.

Tempted by the comparatively moderate charges made in Europe for male and female apparel, most of the passengers had no easy task to get through,

in securing their accumulated trunks when passed by
the investigating Custom House officials.

The luggage brought by us looked quite insignifi-
cant by comparison. A portmanteau, a black bag, a

OUR CONVEYANCE

dispatch-case, and an umbrella, summed up the
Thackerayan *impedimenta*, which, along with my
still more exiguous luggage, were soon hoisted up on
the top of a vehicle of the most primitive type. My
outline of it, hastily done in crayon, will give a
notion of its quaint internal anatomy. Its cramped

space ill-suited the long limbs which tried vainly to accommodate themselves within it, and a grin pervaded the English humorist's face as he scanned its marvellous fittings of leather straps which served as back-rests. Before closing the door four dollars each was demanded by the rapacious driver; and when he was thus satisfied, the glorious sunset and its accompanying twin rainbow having made way by this time for dusk and for twinkling lights, we bumped into Boston by circuitous routes, till we reached the hospitable shelter of the "Tremont House," where quarters had been secured beforehand for us.

A gratulatory supper was soon put before us, and the kindly greeting of Mr. Fields in this huge banqueting-room—which we had at this late hour to ourselves, till joined suddenly by our friend Mr. Arthur Clough—made amends in its cheering prospect for our somewhat forlorn arrival.

The great feature was a large dish of oysters, one of which Thackeray took up on his fork-end, and glancing at it said it must have resembled the right ear of Malchus when cut off, as recorded in Holy Writ. Feeling somewhat oppressed by the banquet, Mr. Fields suggested, as a *finale* and sedative, the straw-tickled sherry-cobbler. For this we adjourned to the smoking-room. Thus began the series of

feastings in superabundance, which afterwards made
the chief recipient describe his American tour as
resulting in one unbroken "indigestion."

We retired to well-earned rest. Next morning,
on comparing notes, we agreed that the beds seemed
to us to have rocked, and that wave-breaks still
acted as a lullaby in our sleep; Thackeray going so
far as to aver that he had actually tumbled out of
bed in the lurches of imagination.

In trying to recall first impressions as they
struck us newcomers in this land of kith and kin, I
seem to have been chiefly exercised by the precocity
of youthful callings, mostly tending to the acquisition
of knowledge, and, along with it, the craving for
intelligent mental pleasures: in the first instance, as
exemplified in the typical newsboy, who did not,
as with us, din with ear-shrieking sounds the latest
news from the pavement; he simply made his way
straight into drawing-room or hotel parlour with his
batch of "'*Eralds* and *Tribunes*," which once handed
to the purchasers, he went off, as a capitalist brat
of eight years of age. When you turned to the
reader of the said papers, you found he was a lad
scarcely in his teens, already devouring the toughest
leaders, and mastering the news of the world
whilst whiffing his cigar, and not without making
shies at a huge expectorator close at hand.

young America.   Boston. nov..

Thackeray showed these graphic efforts of mine to limn their features to guests of his, assembled at the "Tremont" at this time, as I tried my hand at carving an enormous turkey, my first indoctrination in dissection of such huge wings and drumsticks. Notwithstanding the bird's Eastern name, the assembled company, I recollect, gave it a Western origin, and stated —I make no doubt, truly—that this favorite Christmas fare originally came, as it still continued to do, from Virginia.

'ERALD & TRIBUNE'
Dec 29.th 52. Boston !
Latest by the Utopia. 2 cents : —

They good-naturedly acknowledged the general truth of the designs, in the lulls of mastication.

As yet those masterly sketches which delight us

THE "POET BUNN"

in American illustrated works, with such astonishing wealth of observation and with such skilful draughts-manship, had not appeared, or I might have found my critics more difficult to please.

I forget whether amongst the scratches was the one now included, representing the well-known figure of

the impresario Bunn, the "poet Bunn" of *Punch*. This
popular librettist was at the "Revere House," where
we paid him a visit. Like mine host, he had come to
lecture in the States—on his stage experiences. In
the published character-drawings of him, including the
well-known Titmarshian ones, he was attired in fault-
less evening costume. Here he is seen *en déshabille*.
It was on a Sunday, I recollect, after church hours,
and his prayer-book was on the table, and beside it a
refreshing B. and S. tumbler. Beckoning to the one, he
said, "Here is business;" and to the other, "Here is
pleasure." This was not said with any irreverence,
as this curt sentence might suggest. The man, in
the midst of much frolicsome spirit, was really of a
serious and religious frame of mind, exemplified in
his later days by his turning a devout Roman Catholic
and dying in the odour of sanctity at Boulogne-sur-
Mer, where he spent his last breath.

In the same hotel we next visited the famous
prima donna Madame Sontag. Here is her graceful
appearance, to which feeble justice is done, but which
may pass as the pictorial parting record of a world-
famed cantatrice. She was then engaged in farewell
touring concerts. She spoke in mellifluous French:
talked of the Jenny Lind successes before her own,
scarcely expecting to rival the enormous profits made
by that popular songstress, but still with the prospect

of realizing a competence ; then, waving her hand
across her throat, announced to her visitor her in-

tention of closing her *gosier* after her present tour.
With her, as in the case of too many faces met

in those now remote days, it has to be recorded that
Fate, in the shape of some malarious attack, closed
for ever her public career long before it could have
been said to have run its natural course. A sketch
of her as she appeared at this time, and her hand-
gesture expressing her above-mentioned determination
to retire, may be accepted as perhaps the last illustration taken of the features of Countess Rossi. The
"Melodeon" (p. 41) was the handsome concert hall at
that time; we went to hear the famous songstress there.
Thackeray, who was to lecture there a month later,
took note of the acoustic capabilities of the hall, and
ascertained the proper voice-pitch needed.

Mr. Fields has amused his readers by giving his
version of this occasion, when Thackeray, who sat
beside him, volunteered to give imaginary readings of
character of each person as they took their seats in the
stalls near us. When Mr. Fields, who knew everybody,
afterwards told us the real life of those so playfully
described, these readings were found to be in most
cases much nearer the reality than the usual guesses of
palmists or phrenologists. These wiseacres may be said
not to see much farther into character than yonder
wooden sailor seen perched on a supporting bracket on
the Boston Quay, making believe to take an observation with a sham sextant on a non-existent sun.

In old and new guide-books, when compared

together, the striking change is noticed in the fashion
of hotel resorts. Thus we are informed that the claims,
then paramount, of the "Tremont" and the "Revere"

ON THE COMMERCIAL WHARF, BOSTON

hotels, have succumbed to those of yet more splendid
ones, called the "Vendôme" and the "Brunswick." In
the fifties the "Tremont" was new, clean, and full

of comforts, with an abundant *cuisine* of the best—
whether (as we sometimes did) availing yourself of the
special room set apart for repasts of persons having
lady friends with them, or in the more numerously
attended general *table d'hôte.* I recollect at this last

AT THE " TREMONT "

resort, when coming in rather late, taking inadvert-
ently a vacant seat at a side table. I had soon a
gasping sense of gulping down my food too rapidly, as
active waiters plied one, without intervals of rest,
with successive dishes. On demanding the explanation of this unwonted expedition, and expressing a

Boston from Bunkers Hill - Dec 1852

wish for a temporary respite, I was informed this was "an express table" for people anxious to catch a train and with few minutes to spare in degustation. I carefully avoided it in future; I feel sure I should otherwise have succumbed to liver complaint.

The latest victim to this dire and insidious malady was the great orator Daniel Webster. All the streets were, at this period, festooned with mourning draperies, his funeral having taken place on the 29th of October. The papers were filled with panegyrics of his career. One of his greatest flights of oratory, it was then averred, was on the occasion of the inauguration of the Quincy granite pillar, 221 feet high, better known as the Bunker Hill Monument, ten years before his death. I naturally went to inspect it, crossing the Charlestown Ferry for that purpose. I here give the outline of the pleasant prospect of Boston from that place, though probably ulterior conflagrations and demolitions may have quite altered its aspect since then.

Of that stern fight two relics, as noted afterwards
in the first chapter of "The Virginians," were suspended at that time in the library of William Hickling
Prescott, the historian. They have, since his death,
been transferred to the Massachusetts Library as a
bequest. They were the swords of two relatives of

W. H. PRESCOTT

the historian, fighting on opposite
sides at the neighbouring Port of
Charlestown; the naval hero's
name, on the Royal side, was Captain John Linzee, grandfather of
Mrs. Prescott; the other, his oppo-
nent, was Col. William Prescott,
grandfather of the author. W. H.
Prescott only lived half a dozen
years after the time of our meeting

him, having a graceful eulogium paid him by his
English friend. Most of the likenesses of him
were full-faced, besides being youthful ones; here
is his profile, in which his blindness is not noticeable. In his conversation he made you forget this
misfortune by his cheery and bland way of looking
at life. I am glad to have caught its semblance.
It brings back to mind the cosy library. His
wading through old records, aided by his secretary,
was portentous; but this did not dull his bright view
of men and things, which suited your humour as his

clothes did the weather. 'Tis said, I know not with what truth, his overcoats were all labelled as suited for certain degrees of temperature, and were donned accordingly when he sallied forth under the guidance of his secretary. He was what we call an Ultra-Conservative, there known under the pleasing appellation of "Old Hunker." In height and gait Professor Fawcett, who conquered fame also by indomitable pluck against the same calamity, reminded me of his tall erect figure strolling out hitched to the elbow of his amanuensis.

GEORGE TICKNOR

Belonging also to the same euphoniously named party was George Ticknor, historian of Spanish literature, whose companion physiognomy is here inserted. Here, again, in his home, were rows of well-ordered bookshelves. One evening—I recollect, it was after the "Congreve" lecture—we were hospitably invited to adjourn to Mr. Ticknor's house for a sociable chat over pipes and baccy. *À propos* of "pipes" and their introduction into the lecture of the evening, someone asked what they really meant, and what was the Pipe Office. Mr. Ticknor took down from one of his well-supplied shelves a technological dictionary—Spelman's, I think—from which he read

out the following explanation :—" So called because
the papers were kept in a large pipe or cask."

But since that time, in the *édition de luxe* of
Thackeray's works published in 1879, a full number

Expectations.   Charleston. 1853.

of annotations appear to throw doubts upon this
meaning, and the perplexed reader is allowed to
choose whichever version he pleases. This fully
justifies the reticence of the author, who only nodded
in partial acquiescence in the proposed reading of
the word by his friend Mr. Ticknor.

Difficulties hereafter might occur if trusting to
conflicting lexicographers. For example, they allude

to pipes, they dilate upon tobacco, but the useful
receptacles for the moistening results, popularly
known as "spittoons," or "expectorators," or "expect-
aroons," are terms jealously excluded from their

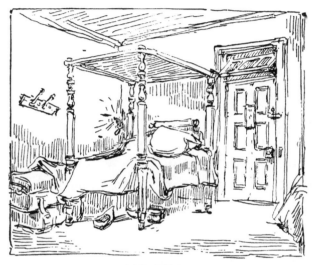

A SPLASHY BED

vocabularies; yet they are palpable enough to the
senses. The courtyard of the Charleston Hotel was
piled with these in the morning, when the wholesome
water-hose was turned upon them vigorously, a sight
quite unique in its way. This, however, is in antici-
pation of events.

Insufficient, strange to say, they were, for I recollect being put into a bedroom the walls of which
were maculated with the bistre-coloured emissions of
former slumberers on the same pillow.

3

On the 16th of November, and in pleasant balmy
weather, we left Boston for New York, after a week's
stay. We took the cars at eight o'clock in the morning, and I was duly laden with a lot of heavy
brass checks corresponding to others fixed to our luggage, each label being suspended to a leather strap.

Thackeray has described a scene which I here
illustrate in outline, though unconscious, as I saw
it, of the bygone memories it personally evoked in
his person, of which he afterwards, in the preface to
the New York edition of his works, made the New
York public, and therefore the whole reading world,
a confidant. It was when " a rosy-cheeked little peri-
patetic book-merchant " accosted him with his own

" THACKERAY'S WORKS, SIR ! "

volumes, and called out "Thackeray's Works!" quite
unaware that he was addressing the author himself.
He therefore re-read his "Shabby Genteel Story," of
a dozen years before, as we were whisked along the
undulating territory of Massachusetts. I expended
twenty-five cents in the purchase of "Uncle Tom's
Cabin," and was properly harrowed by the tale told
by Mrs. Beecher-Stowe. But Thackeray declined to
plunge into its tale of woe; his opinion expressed upon
it being that stories founded upon such painful themes
were scarcely within the legitimate purview of story-
telling. Besides, judicious friends had dinned well
into his ears the propriety of his not committing
himself to either side of the Slavery Question, then a
burning one, if he wished his career as a lecturer
not to become a burthen to him.

He dwelt in preference upon the blithe aspects of
American life, such as the group of children in the
cars, eight in number, every one of whom he wished
there and then to present with a dollar tip a-piece.
Their conversation was of the outspoken sort, so we
soon learnt their tribulations, the most serious of
which was having forgotten to bring with them a
cake prepared for the journey. Jimmy, the white-
hatted youngster, evidently felt the loss acutely. But
when we were crossing the ferry the cake was replaced
by another, soon sliced up and devoured.

D 2

Meanwhile the train went on at a good speed, with intermittent stoppages. At one of the stations, where an appetising lunch was set out, to which I was doing full justice, not hearing the departure signal, I only got on the platform in time to see the

A GROUP OF CHILDREN

receding engine and cars speeding on and leaving me solitary on the platform. The metal labels seemed to weigh heavier somehow in my pocket as I suddenly realised to myself the discomfort caused to the owner of the baggage in not having these vouchers forthcoming on arrival in New York.

I came on by a slow train, known technically as an "accommodation" one, which stopped at every station, and brought me some time later to New York.

I got out, and, having gone some distance, inquired for the " Clarendon Hotel." " Second block," was the reply, and it dawned upon me that the direction referred, not to the streets, but to the divisions between each of them, a sensible innovation.

IN THE ACCOMMODATION TRAIN

Thackeray had extricated the traps by merely pointing them out, but with imperturbable good-humor and kindness made the best of the mishap. Besides, he had been amused by the advent of a well-known character, making his appearance, upon his arrival, as an interviewer, as he did to most European celebrities, with a view to "copy." More welcome was a more genuine chronicler, who was only second in visiting rotation, the historian Mr.

Bancroft, whom I found already in converse with
him. He had what the French call the nose-pincher
kind of spectacles ; over his forehead was the
Napoleonic wisp of hair, and the air of diplomacy
suffused his sallow features. It was only in conversa-

tion, and by his references
to literary Hinterland recol-
lections, that you guessed him
to be older than he looked.
For example, at dinner he said
he had met Lord Byron once
at Genoa. A reference to the
pages of Thomas Moore shows
this must have been as far
back as the November of
1822, when Byron was oc-

MR. BANCROFT

cupying his Villa Saluzzo, at Albano. Thackeray
said he was then at Charterhouse. Mr. Bancroft
lectured one evening before the New York Historical
Society, where we went to hear him. He sought
relaxation from his historical labours by inviting
friends in the evening, and a night or two after our
arrival Thackeray came back to the hotel, where I
had remained solitarily, and described astonishing
feats he had been witness to for the first time.

This was his initiation into the table-turning
mystery, the hat-twirling, etc., accompanied by spirit-

MR. BANCROFT'S LECTURE

rapping manifestations: a nine days' wonder, or rather
more. Whilst the mania lasted Mr. Home was the hero
of the hour. If we believe his published Memoirs—
which, by the bye, are singularly reticent as to his
stay in New York—at this period he was only twenty
years of age, though looking older. Here he may

TABLE-TURNING

be seen jotting down the alphabetical raps, whilst the
rest of the company, finger-tips touching each other,
keep up the current of spiritual enunciation. Some
words came out, wondrously distorted if names, and
misspelt if mere words. It is to be feared that some
maliciously disposed votaries on these occasions used

to give him linguistic nuts to crack which were beyond his limited comprehension.

Belonging to the noble New England army of authors may here be mentioned the Rev. Theodore Parker, the Anti-Slavery champion and eloquent

THE REV. THEODORE PARKER PREACHING

preacher. Though his home was at Boston, I first heard him lecture at the New York Tabernacle, full of fire and earnestness, quite refreshing to listen to. The audience was sufficiently crowded, though the syllabus was as alarming as the title of Bossuet's

"Histoire Universelle." The subject was "The Progress of Mankind." The reading requisite for such a theme was prodigious. Primitive man and his latest developments came under review. Franklin was belauded for teaching lightning to go straight, and not to destroy everything, as it did in its "rowdy days"—an illu-

Horace Greeley. 1842.

sion which tickled the groundlings. On the whole it may be said that poor old Europe came in s e c o n d · b e s t. After the great names of Lawrence and Lowell had been justly singled out as grand New England worthies, a Cockney was a little ruffled at finding "Chicopee and London" bracketed together as towns emblematic of advanced civilisation. London came second after a miniature Manchester with barely twelve thousand inhabitants; but then it was in Massachusetts.

The mention of Franklin brings to mind Horace Greeley, happily dubbed "a later Franklin" by the poet Whittier. He was a welcome visitor at the "Clarendon," and in a few sentences helped one somewhat out of the tangled maze of American politics, and was a good type of the Press militant. I was able in after-years to return the compliment by answering interrogations as to affairs in Europe when I met him in Paris. I remember seeing him at an English charity ball given there. He was much exercised, on asking me to point out to him which of the ladies were the noble patronesses whose titles figured on the list of the evening's programme, at being informed that they so appeared *pro formâ* only, not many being present on that occasion. He had, at that time, quite recovered from his Presidential Election fatigues in 1852, when his party, whom we should denominate Conservatives, but who in the States were known as the " Whigs," were " dished."

On the 12th of November, by telegrams from Halifax announcing that Thackeray was a passenger on board the *Canada*, etc. etc., Thackeray's arrival in New York had been heralded with the usual flourish of trumpets, in which the *New York Daily Tribune* chiefly distinguished itself. It said, under the date of November 13th, " He comes on the invitation of the Mercantile Library Association. The Merchants' Clerks of New York aspire to the culture of scholars and gentlemen, and import from abroad—

not the latest teacher of double entry, but the most thoughtful critic of manners and society, the subtlest humorist, and the most effective, because the most genial, satirist the age has known. . . . Terminus, once rightly reckoned the sacredest of gods, must at this rate be soon left without a worshipper." This was written by Mr. Henry James, the father of the well-known author and dramatist now amongst us. He and Mr. Dana and Professor Felton were a few of the able staff supporting the paper. The editor, and part owner of its stock, was Mr. Horace Greeley, whose presses we went over to examine one afternoon.

Centre market.
new york.
April 1853. S. C.

CHAPTER II

AFTER an active morning spent in interviews and
business, we took the Bowery tramcars, which dropped
us not far from 548, Broadway, near Prince Street,
where we met by appointment Mr. Millard Felt, who
showed us over the Rev. Mr. Chapin's Unitarian
Chapel, from which the Rev. Henry
Bellows had lately retired as pastor.
It was called the Church of the
Unity. I shall not easily forget the
author's expression of wonder when
he looked athwart the long, dark,
wainscoted benches, and saw the pil-
lared nave and the oak pulpit. He
seemed fascinated by the idea of his
lay-sermonising in this place. Then

THE REV. H. BELLOWS

looking at the communion table, and appealing to
Secretary Felt, he asked—"Would not the sacred

emblems be removed from the altar?" followed by
the query: "Will the organ strike up when I enter?"
Then, peering into the side room, he further inquired—
"I suppose I shall have to enter by the sacristy?"
To sum up the matter, it was determined that this
was the eligible resort. The announcements were
made as follows :—

LECTURES TO BE GIVEN ON THE FOLLOWING EVENINGS

Fridays—19th November.	Mondays—22nd November.
26th "	29th "
3rd December.	6th December.

At 8 o'clock.

Price :—3 Dollars for the Course.

The subscription list was closed on Thursday evening, but the rush for tickets soon made it clear that
a second course would be necessary, and this was
also announced thus :—

Wednesday, December 1st.	Monday, December 13th.
Tuesday, " 7th.	Wednesday, " 15th.
Friday, " 10th.	Friday, " 17th.

filling up nearly a month's interval of time.

The accompanying illustration (frontispiece), jotted
down at the time from a back bench in the row of open
seats, gives an idea of the prospect. The lecturer
ascended the somewhat high rostrum, which had been
erected fronting the pulpit; along with him came the
secretary, Mr. Millard Felt, who, on the warm greetings

of welcome subsiding, introduced the lecturer in a few well-chosen sentences, and sat down on a chair at the side. All went cheerily to the end. As was the case in England, the reporters had been asked not to give *in extenso* or even too liberally the subject-matter of the lectures. This intent was honourably adhered to; but to eke out their paragraphs—which Thackeray read with interest the next morning—the manipulation of his coat-tails, varied with his favourite posture of diving his hands in his side-pockets, was dwelt upon facetiously, as well as the unusual fact that he indulged in no particular form of gesticulation. The first and only intimation anyone had that these humoristic details tickled the author's fancy was on the arrival in New York in mid-January, a month after date, of the January number of *Fraser's Magazine*, containing his unsigned, yet palpably his own, description of this quaint form of personal characterisation.

Neither the prevailing gloom of the place (the lights, as usual wherever there is dark wainscot, proving powerless to diffuse brightness), nor inclement weather, such as that on the occasion of the second lecture, could daunt the intrepid ladies and gentle-men, the *élite* of New York fashion, from coming and applauding throughout the double courses.

Amidst the applause and the enthusiasm caused by Thackeray's special address on the closing of the first course, viz., on the evening of the 6th of December, resolutions were proposed and seconded by Mr. Kelly, President of the Board of Education, and Mr. Osgood, presiding at this juncture. The latter, I recollect, said: "I don't like telling tales out of school, but a friend of mine told me Mr. Thackeray said he only found Englishmen here; he begged to say that in Mr. Thackeray they discovered a genuine Yankee." (Tremendous shouts of applause.) Mr. Kelly in his speech seconded the resolution.

As far as memory serves after this lapse of time, the citizenship of New York was then bestowed upon the author—a high distinction. The other resolutions carried referred to the great satisfaction given by his visit, and gave expression to the thanks due to the Mercantile Association, of which Mr. Millard Felt on this occasion was the chairman, and his fellow-committee-men were Messrs. Francis Hawks and George Moore.

The next day's papers, December 7th, contained a report of these proceedings, which divided the attention of their readers with the lengthy annual address to Congress by President Fillmore. A fillip was given to the sale of the original works descanted on in the lectures, and such paragraphs as these were numerous in the advertisements of the time:—
"Bangs, Brothers and Co. issue, wholesale and retail,

8vo editions of Addison, Thackeray, Steele," etc. etc.

The limp brown-covered "Esmond" reprints were sold for the trifling sum of 50 cents per copy; not, however—to the writer's chagrin—in Queen Anne type, but in the ordinary type, and, if I mistake not, with the new-fangled American spelling of words, quite transmogrifying its appearance. These drawbacks were, however, counterbalanced; for the reprints had the effect of popularising the author, who was assailed by demands for his discourses.

PRESIDENT FILLMORE

The now transpontine suburb of Brooklyn came in for the next engagement. I went; not as is now done, across the wide expanse of river by a level bridge—one of the wonders of modern engineering—but by taking the Fulton ferry-boat, price one cent. The view of New York and its numerous steeple-topped roofs was very grand from the water, with its array of merchant-ships, clippers, and liners. Here is an attempt to give an idea of it, but it needs the adjunct of tender melting-blue distances to realise the scene.

4

NEW YORK, FROM BROOKLYN

The steep ascent of the Main Street was at this time lined with non-splendid houses, the worse for wear. In one of these, and midway up, I climbed up some rickety stairs, and gave the lecture-announcement to a clerk at a desk, who copied it out, and, scarcely moving from his seat, handed the slip of paper to the type-setter. In a trice I had the proofs in hand, which were forwarded to other newspapers, and soon the lecturer found himself addressing an intelligent audience in one of the halls, of which I regret that I forget the name. It was the privilege of a certain number of the clergy of this district to grace the lecture by their presence, and their white chokers gave a solemnity of the Quaker order to the scene. At the jovial supper which followed the lecture this somewhat starched demeanour was replaced by boisterous hilarity. It is an odd circumstance that, whilst genuine humour often evanesces, the figments of the Joe-Millerian type keep fast hold on the memory. Such an one belongs to this evening's entertainment, and elicited laughter. A country bumpkin, who had never seen either a negro or a cigar, was asked by a smoker of that swarthy breed whether he would whiff a Havannah. His reply was: "Na, na, Mr. Deil, I canna eat fire like you!" This evening's reception was, if need were, a satisfying proof to Thackeray that he would meet with appreciative listeners wherever he appeared, irrespective of the specially chosen agencies for promoting popularity.

Amongst the friends of student-time in Paris I now met at the "Century" Club was a clever landscape painter, Kensett, who had grown as stout as he was formerly the reverse, and who didn't recognise me in the least, owing to some facial change of the same nature. We met at an artistic gathering called the "Sketch Club," the assembled company coming together with no other designs than to chat, smoke, and, last, not least, eat oysters of the usual huge size.

Church, then emerged already into fame, was painting scenes of the grandiose kind : such as the Falls of Niagara, very skilfully done—his speciality.

But the host of able painters from the United States who watched and who studied the very latest phases of French art were, as a body, only then in embryo. I understand, from the publications devoted to art, that the great demand now is for works of the ultra-Impressionist school, not even

thought of at that time. On the contrary, the
polished prettinesses of the Düsseldorf artists filled
galleries of their own, and had a ready sale, whilst
in the South many filled their walls with elaborate
copies from the old masters. Native talent has made
prodigious strides since then.

On Thanksgiving Day—I believe, always fixed for
the last Thursday of November, on this occasion the
25th—I tested my powers of perambulation, but I
found, like the gentleman returning home after excessive potations, it was not so much the length as the
breadth of the way
that was fatiguing.
The perpetual zig-
zagging from one
object or place of
interest to another
makes the journey
from end to end of
Broadway no small
effort.

From some per-
verse feeling I
longed for a mo-
ment to be whisked
off in one of the
numerous well-

appointed private carriages which wait patiently at houses whilst the owners are calling, and the smart black coachman and his companion sit on the box-seat in well-drilled immutability.

Hotels in every stage of incompleteness—such as the "Lafarge," then with gaping brick walls and no frontage, only posters with prospective enjoyments held forth of every description, as per sketch (amongst them the Bateman children in *The Young Couple*, whom I saw, little dreaming that here were to be much-cherished relatives, and the "Leah" of fame to become my dear brother's wife thereafter)—and fully-equipped brand-new resorts, like the "Metro-politan," with covers and mitre-shaped napkins laid for 200 guests seated at one or two long tables.

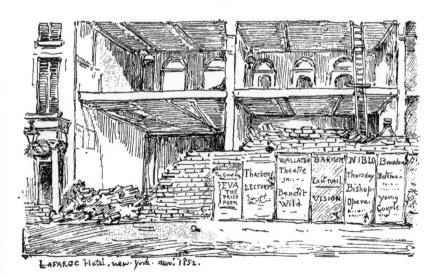

LAFARGE Hotel. new-york. nov. 1852.

A row of negro servants, brush in hand, used to be seen sitting on a bench in the entrance hall of the hotels. As the visitors came down, each of them, in rotation, seized the coat-collar and dusted it, flicking the brush over the whole attire of the owner, who was

THE BRUSHING PROCESS

thus made smart for the day. Specialists, such as the "hat-negro" and the "elevator-man," were at that time unknown, and are quite modern developments of the "help."

Another sumptuous store of white marble was Stewart's haberdashery shop. This we sketched too; but the sketch, true then, is no longer so; the store and the goods have moved up town. The noble

THE BROADWAY

owner's body has been snatched, and, I regret to say,
I am unaware whether he was ever recovered from
the clutches of these ghouls.

At right angles with the great thoroughfare is
Wall Street. The sketch on page 78 shows its
former semblance, with overhead telegraph wires. I
recollect going up one of the stairs of a house in it,
and, instead of finding the man I wanted, I saw a
scrap of paper fastened to the door by two pins,
stating laconically—"Gone to Europe; back in a
few days." I believe this is not a bad indication
of the rapid go-ahead mode of business here.

Broadway is in its full length two and a half miles,

extending from Union Square to the Battery, and
giving the gentleman-lounger (the Titmarshian version
of the French *flâneur*) a very fair idea of the city's
trades, hotels, amusements, bars, etc.   New to us
then, but familiarised to Cockney-land by its adoption
in London, was the labour-saving system of com-
bining in one person the conductor and driver of

THE BROADWAY OMNIBUS

the omnibus, with its interior intimation—" Children
taking seats full fare."   In order to fulfil an appointment made with Barnum's chief business agent,
Mr. Le Grand Smith, to meet Barnum at his museum,
Thackeray took seats in one of these popular vehicles,
fondly fancying we should go in a straight line.   But
the pavement was torn up, cobble or flint stone
making way for granite stones; soon again, the wags

asserted, to be once more uprooted to insert iron rails.
This necessitated such constant divergence into off-
streets, that walking was obviously a speedier method
of transit. The sunny side of Broadway was bright
and cheerful, the sky beautifully blue overhead, and a
clear atmosphere so exhilarating to the spirits that
when we at last reached and entered Barnum's
museum the contrast of grime and gloom there pervading—as is often the case in haunts made to be
viewed by gas-light—only made the scene more than
usually dismal.

There were stuffed quadrupeds in plenty; there
were sallow wax figures, prominent amongst which
memory recalls the groups of Lord Byron, surrounded
by his Missolonghi bodyguard of ferocious Suliotes,
arrayed in faded tinselled costumes; also, further on,
some Chinese notabilities were lying prone, with their

effigy heads off their shoulders, not, as is too often
the case in Celestial
annals, after decapitation,
but here only temporarily
deprived of their head-
pieces for the purposes of
cleaning. English relics,
such as the signed copy
of "Magna Charta," and

SEAL-TIGER

BARNUM'S MUSEUM

the huge coach which once bore Queen Adelaide on
gala days, were conspicuous.   Two semi-somnolent
creatures attracted you—one being a "seal-tiger," rolling his eyes in wonderment at such matutinal visitors,
and the other its black keeper, whose special function it

was to rouse the dormant amphibian lying in its straw lair, and whose eyes also revolved in the gloom. We had used up these sensations, and had sat down in a small office the walls of which were hung round with daguerrotypes of General Tom Thumb leaning majestically upon the shoulders of Barnum, when the latter gentleman entered and introduced himself to us.

This interview has escaped notice in that great showman's Memoirs. He wished for Thackerayan collaboration in the first number, then coming out, of an illustrated paper in imitation of the *London News*. And who knows what f u r t h e r developments flitted across that fertile brain in connection with the English author's visit to America? Thackeray

Barnum.

said he wished to maintain his own personal independence of movement, scarcely compatible with the big-drum methods involved in monster speculative schemes. He courteously declined to write his impressions.

My description of the museum refers altogether to that of forty years ago. The show disappeared in lambent flames one day, only to rise up elsewhere—a fate shared in by the great impresario's palace of "Iranistan." But these disasters never daunted this master-spirit. Subsequently, on Thanksgiving Day, I happened to pass by the museum, which was thronged with people entering it. A placard was put up— " Beware of Pickpockets "—a warning not needless, as a little incident which I witnessed there and then seemed to show. Sitting on a stool in the gangway

BARNUM'S AGENT

was a purblind sailor, with his c o p p e r - b o x on his knees, a further appeal to the c h a r i t a b l e being a picture of a ship struck by lightning, the same flash depriving him of his sight. A kind p a s s e r - b y flung down a contribution, which an u n s c r u p u l o u s thief tried to grab hold of, when suddenly a little t e r r i e r hidden b e h i n d the blind man's coat-tails dashed for- ward to the rescue, and discomfited the would-be purloiner.

At another street-corner of Broadway was to be seen the liquor-seller, dealing out drinks, chiefly of soda-water and ginger-beer, at the moderate charge of three cents per tumbler ; or, taking it in the gross, at the reduced rate of " forty soda-water tickets for a dollar," as the wayfarer was informed by a placard. The briskness with which these refreshing beverages were distributed, gushing through brilliant metallic

DRINKS

dolphin-shaped spouts, evinced their popularity, and must have been highly remunerative to this bearded liquor-trader. We give here his likeness as he stood behind his open-air bar.

It will not escape the acute observer that this worthy wears a chimney-pot hat, the great emblem of

JOHN N. GENIN'S HAT STORE

equality, and hence its popularity in the States. Two years before this time, the Jenny Lind *furore* in New

York was manifested at the outset by a tremendous
rush for tickets at Mr. Barnum's gallery in Broadway.
The boxes were put up to auction to the highest
bidder, and, to the horror of the "Swedish Nightin-
gale," she noticed suspended over her own private box
a gigantic-sized broad-brim.   This sacred retreat of
the prima donna had been won, as highest bidder, by
Mr. Genin (here is his likeness), the great hatter.
The moderate outlay of 140 dollars had secured this
splendid advertisement.   Possibly with an eye to fur-
thering the headgear trade, and with his manifest love
for large headpieces, he wrote a letter to Thackeray,
expressing his wish to acknowledge his indebtedness
to the author for the pleasure derived from perusing his
works by presenting him with a hat, also stating that
he had an uncomfortable feeling in the reflection that
the author could receive no benefit from the purchase
of his books, and asking to discharge his part of the
national debt by furnishing his head with all external
ornament it might require whilst in his country.   I
quite forget whether the wish was acceded to by
Thackeray, but, as a salve, I fancy he asked me to
have my measure taken in his stead.   The wonderful
instrument for measuring the cranium—which I first
saw here—was applied to my occiput and frontal bone ;
but, alas! when the hat was produced, my bumps or
something else proved rebellious, and I was scared at

seeing my personal appearance thus, when looking in the glass.

This machine is of Italian invention, is manufactured in Paris, and is known as the "conformateur." It has been improved upon of late years.

TAKING YOUR MEASURE

It may be added that a reference to the later American preface written for the reprints of his works by Thackeray, showed conclusively that the worthy hatter was in error in attributing niggardliness to the American publishers, who, on the contrary, are there stated to have behaved most handsomely, especially the Messrs. Appleton firm.

THE RESULT

Whilst on the subject of reprints, and his lament at the mutilation of some stories, such as the omission of the first chapter in the "Little Dinner at Timmins's" (supposed by some to be due to its phrasing, as to "Lady Bungay weighing two of Blanche, even when she is not in the f——," as some wag hinted), or, worse still, the unearthing some of his early bantlings which he wished buried in oblivion, it may now be said that the author was too severe upon himself, and that we now like to have these recondite fugitive pieces brought to light once more, as has been the case lately with some such by a literary society of our own, though only for private circulation.

Though somewhat out of proper sequence of time, it may be here added that the whole series of red-covered little books was brought back to England, and, on explanation to the Liverpool Customs agent, suffered to be retained, being thereafter a useful record to consult *en bloc* when questions arose as to what to publish or what to omit in this country in future editions.

The next emporium of the book-trade in New York is Messrs. Harpers', where we penetrated into the inner or business sanctum, and, when seated, after the usual amenities and introductory greeting were over, we had leisure to scan the shrewd features of Mr. James Harper, then chief director of this great publishing house. The other brother-partners we did not see at this time—indeed, the apartment was purposely small and snug, not admitting of large receptions and of general converse. The sketch gives the aspect of

5

the place, on the shelves being conspicuous the Thackerayan reprints and other popular authors. Presently a lithe little girl came in, and was formally introduced by the father to Thackeray. He shook

AT HARPERS'

hands with her, and, smiling, said, " So this is a ' pirate's ' daughter, is it ? " an appellation which tickled the enterprising publisher's sense of humour into an approving grin. Thackeray ventured to ask him whose name stood foremost in popularity in book sales in the United States. He good-naturedly took down a ponderous ledger, turned up the leaves at letter J, and said, "George Payne Rainsford James heads the list, far ahead of any other author, as you can judge for yourself by glancing at the number of his books sold. He turns out a novel every six months, and the success is always the same, and tremendous." This was an "eye-opener," to use a trans-Atlantic phrase. When asked to explain the reason of this immense hold upon the public, the reply was prompt: "The main reason is that his romances can always be safely placed upon the family table, with the certainty that no page will sully or call the blush to the cheek of any member of the household." Well was he named in former days by Thackeray, "that teeming parent of romance." There was, however, a rift in his literary lute. Though Consul at that time at Norfolk, Virginia (a place omitted from our wanderings), the fact that in some early performance he had faintly hinted his disapproval of slavery—this alone · made the worthy Norfolkians hostile, and presently he exchanged the States for Venice, the only place where he could not descry two muffled cavaliers ascending a hill on horseback.

The Harper firm had launched the monthly bearing their name, a year or two before this time, on its tide of success. This caused others to follow the same course, with less satisfactory results, ending by crippling for long days those connected with them.

This was the case with *Putnam's Monthly*, which was delightful reading in its first years. Here is the profile of G. W. Curtis, its brilliant editor. When we knew him he had hyacinthine locks and a shaven face, exchanged in later years for a white - bearded physiognomy. I regretted to see his name in a recent New York obituary notice. He had paid a graceful tribute to Thackeray, recalling these social pleasures in America, in the first volume of his periodical.

G. W. CURTIS

Boston, the Athens of America, and nursery of many illustrious scribes, now claimed to have its lecturing innings also. So thither we went, making raids, besides, on neighbouring capitals. One of these was forty-four miles off by rail, *i.e.*, Providence, Rhode Island. The journey was easy, the audience large and appreciative. This was on December 22nd, when nights were getting chilly. It was therefore a little rough upon those fond of their cheerful cigar, to be compelled, as most of them were, to content themselves with a discussion on the benefits conferred upon that State by liquor laws prohibiting the sale of alcoholic drinks. Everybody, I noticed, went to bed early. I only sketched a pair of blüchers, whose shadow was cast upon the sleeper's room-door outside, at the hotel. I can therefore only mention Providence *à propos de bottes.*

Boston did not resent coming in second on the list. On the contrary, with evident heartiness and an air

Dec. 22ⁿᵈ Providence.'52.

of literary confraternity, Thackeray was welcomed and relished, as he had been by the select and cultured audiences of his own country. A few cantankerous members of the press were adverse, 'tis true; but they may be pardoned, as they were the originating cause of the amusing lucubration sent by Thackeray to *Fraser's Magazine* (appearing in January, 1853), which was a renewal of his old bantering reviews in that publication. Without telling anyone in the States that he had written it, without having his name affixed

to it, when it came to the United States, ten days
after, it was at once recognised as his, and was received with good-humoured laughter by some, but by
others as an unpleasant scarification of the minor
penny-a-lining fraternity.

To while away the leisure moments, we paid
several visits to the museum of pictures in Boston.
Thackeray was much struck—as, indeed, must everyone
be—by the superb portraits of General Washington
and Mrs. Washington by Gilbert Stuart. They seem
to have their charm increased by their unfinished state,
the background being only partially rubbed in. I asked
the committee, through their complaisant secretary,
Mr. C. Folsom, to allow me to copy them, as I thought
the future author of " The Virginians " would like to
have these faces before him in Europe. See how
intentions are baffled ! I painted these, working often
during closing-time, by special grace. I presented them
to Thackeray in New York (he had left me behind at
Boston to give finishing-touches), when, lo ! the great
compliment was paid me of asking to have these
copies copied. Thackeray's friend, Mr. Degan, whose
friendship we had made on board the boat coming
across the Atlantic, took charge of them for that
purpose ; and it was only years afterwards, and
long after the owner's sad departure, that an opportunity occurred of sending them back through the

W.M. THACKERAY. Boston. 1852.

AT THE MELODEON, BOSTON

instrumentality of Thackeray's daughter and her husband, Mr. Leslie Stephen, the distinguished author, when on a visit to the States.

It is not without diffidence I mention the name of Washington Allston, whose reputation was

CUSTOM HOUSE, BOSTON

tremendous in his day. Here, in this museum, was his huge composition of "Belshazzar's Feast"—left incomplete, it is true, yet sufficiently forward to show the painter's ultimate aim and intention. There is a certain Venetian glow and mastery of colour in it

which attracts, but nothing can justify the introduction of such a foreground group as seen there, of
which the faces border on the grotesque. It is in the
art essays he wrote, in his genial conversation, and
in his able correspondence, we must seek, in order to

FROM "BELSHAZZAR'S FEAST"

realise his hold upon his time. We give here the
rough indication of the group alluded to.

There is more sweet pleasure derivable from small,
unpretending canvases in the same collection than in
ambitious compositions. Here, for example, in sober
greys and in sad feature, is the little figure of the ill-
fated authoress, Margaret Fuller-Ossoli, deftly done

by Thomas Hicks. He was a pleasant boon-companion at the "Century" symposium and elsewhere. Besides painting people, chiefly celebrities, he used to mimic them amusingly. His representation of Daniel Webster the orator was very whimsical. Whilst delivering a mock speech of his he would take out a huge red Bandanna handkerchief, and unfolding it deliberately would, after many nose-pullings, at last recover the thread of his discourse, and start afresh on ponderous sentences. It was said to be a good skit on the departed statesman's method of speech.

The proverbially sudden changes of temperature in the States now were realised: one day it was balmy, the next was frosty and snowing—with pantomime rapidity of altering scenes, we had the whole population sleighing. The juvenile portion at Boston preferred "coasting." The old edition of Webster contained this description of it: "The sport of sliding down a hill-side upon sleds or sledges in winter (used in the Eastern States, and also in New Brunswick, where the application of the word may possibly have originated amongst the Acadians—from *côte*, old French *coste*, a hillside)."

The little lads are seen careering down the slopes, helter-skelter. In the distance is seen Faneuil Hall, not the original "Cradle of Liberty," as it was called,

"COASTING.— The sport of sliding down a hill side upon sleds or sledges in winter. (Used in the Eastern States, & also in New Brunswick, where this application of the word being possibly here originated among the Acadians from Côte, or Côté, a hill-side.)— Webster; Pic—

Boston, Jan'ry 6, 1853. E. y. C.

"COASTING"

built by that patriot of Huguenot descent, but the second structure, reared when the first was burned down.

I had by this time finished the two portrait copies of General and Mrs. Washington. I packed them up, and brought them to New York for Thackeray's kind acceptance.

Before leaving Boston I peeped into some of its public buildings and institutions; one of these was the Boston Sessions. I forget what exact business was transacted at this court of justice. The Sessions are generally held for granting licences to innkeepers, etc., and for laying out highways. They answer seemingly

AT THE BOSTON SESSIONS

to our petty sessions, though here one magistrate
seems to suffice. A legal document is being read,
which does not seem to interest the public at large.

— A Glimpse of 'Change. New-york . Dec 52. —

They in preference gathered in the corridors and
other precincts, not choosing to stay in court, which,
to tell the truth, like others I know of, was close and
stuffy.

After Bostonian amenities came round once more
the mingled bustle and high pressure of New York
amusements and sights.

At right angles with Broadway was Wall Street,
the often-de-
scribed business
centre of New
York, of which
the sketch gives
some notion as
it existed at
that time. As
you entered the
Merchants' Ex-
change in that
thoroughfare
you heard the
voices of eager
auctioneers,
seen gesticulat-
ing, each of
them in their
individual stalls
fixed circularly
round the inner
Rotunda. Map
in hand, he
pointed out the
exact locality of the estate being put up for sale. That
preliminary over, he would take the bids thus:—" 120

dollars " offered ; an advance to " 150 dollars " is bid ; and after increasing volubility the hammer comes down, and successive properties are disposed of in the same manner. This went on till the clock of Trinity Church, hard by, struck three o'clock, when the whole throng dispersed, and with a bare interval I found myself in comparative solitude. Only one tardy clerk was at his

desk casting up his accounts, and a negro sweeper was raising dust-clouds with his broom. Other open-air estate agents are seen, in modest rivalry to Wall Street appraisers, trying to sell estates by placarding the same in the streets. Here, for example, was a lad dressed as a clown, holding a board on a pole. The advertisement ran thus: " A house and lot for two hundred dollars; a chance for a home for life at the village of Maspeth." Neither the motley wear nor the prospect of having a rural retreat in Long Island seemed to fascinate the crowd, which passed on rapidly, and heedless of such tempting opportunities of investment. Perhaps the vocifera-

tions of the Wall Street mart were fatal omissions
here.

Close by these open-air monetary transactions, a
visit to a neighbouring jeweller's store in Broadway

New York. — The close of business in Wall St. Dec - '52. E.C.

CLOSING TIME

will reveal to you how soon gold becomes specie. The
courteous trader informed me—what, indeed, the sign
over the central housetop had certified in a certain
emblematic way, by representing an eagle sustaining
in its beak a tiny repeater—that either Australian or
Californian lucky diggers will come into their store,

to all appearance dire tatter-
demalions. They at once
proceed to haul out of the
recesses of their garments a
gold nugget or two, which
is weighed, and soon bartered
for a lump sum of money.
I remember the firm's twin
name, "Ball and Black." *Per
contra*, no ore of any kind,
I should say, could be found
on the body of the negro

Ball Black & Comp. *new york*

whom I saw, as I came
out of the goldsmiths'
shop, listlessly sitting
upon the chain encircling
the City Hall Park, smok-
ing his weed contentedly:
a dock-loafer, probably.

Amongst the promi-
nent figures of New York
at this season was a
claimant to the Bourbon
throne, who pretended to
be the actual Louis XVII.,
who had escaped from the
Temple during the French

A DOCK-LOAFER

6

Revolutionary turmoil. His real name was the Rev. Eleazar Williams; his usual occupation was that of a missionary amongst the Canadian Indians. For their benefit he had translated the Bible into Mohawk; ill-natured people hinted that he was himself descended from some Iroquois chief, a supposition justified by his reddish-brown complexion and features. The humour of the hour was, however, to greet him with mock obeisances; and the intrepid went so far as to ask to see the documents authenticating his royal parentage, which he invariably brought with him under one arm, whilst in his other hand he grasped —not a sceptre, but the homely gingham. "Our Dauphin" was the title he went by familiarly in New York. It must be supposed that setting up as a Pretender pays; there are so many of them. Ten years before, a couple appeared in the United States, according to Bacourt's amusing Memoirs, pretending to be descendants of the Chevalier Bayard, although that hero never was married! These were, of course, exceptional instances of misdirected hospitality—the base coin which, in spite of careful scrutiny, will get foisted amidst the pure gold of society.

Washington Irving, who, for abbreviation's sake, was known as "Old Knick," from his early work —"The History of New York, by Diedrich Knicker-bocker"—was the most lionised of the notabilities we

A LION'S ENTRÉE

AS A BOURBON PRETENDER

met, whether at balls or elsewhere. There was little sense of lassitude visible in his cheerful face as he sat there chatting with the hostess, in preference choosing a quiet nook away from the dancers and fiddlers. He has in published letters confided, with

l̲ Washington Irving - nov 29ᵗʰ 1852.

mock modesty, to us "that the dances then in vogue put me out of countenance, and are not such as a gentleman of my years should witness." This assumed prudery is as amusing as were the numerous accessories which t e m p o r a r i l y hid the graceful move-ment of the marble nymph near him—in the shape of hats or piles of supper-plates and champagne bottles.

I seem to hear now his mellow, chatty voice, not without a dash of huskiness in it, due to age, when-ever he came for a quiet gossip with Thackeray at the "Clarendon." He would then, albeit venerated by his friend Charles Dickens, not conceal that, beside loyally reciprocated friendship, he had what the French call a "tooth," and we a "grudge," against him, for embittering the two kindred

countries, his own and England, against each other.
This was, of course, before the Bozzian second
visit, in which every misunderstanding was con-

THE REFRESHMENT ROOM

doned, and the hatchet buried in oblivion and
dollars.

The portraits which I have seen of "Geoffrey
Crayon, Gent[n]," as a rule give one his youthful

features and appearance. I should feel regret if, by giving his semblance at this time, I were infringing a tacit desire of his own not to be limned in his declining years. One day—it was on January 17th, my diary states—we met him, when ourselves going from New York to Philadelphia, when, stowing away

a supply of newspapers which he had bought, he briskly conversed the whole time till we parted at the final railway station. He was going to consult archives at Washington, where we again met him.

Thomas Francis Meagher.

In the same way Thackeray met, a few days after, in the railway cars, another interesting figure, that of Thomas Francis Meagher, who whiled away the tedium of the journey by telling us of his thrilling adventures and plucky experiences.

It was interesting to see this impromptu meeting of the now genial rebel and the author of the "Battle of Limerick," written in *Punch* in 1848, and to think of its well-known lines :—

" Then we summoned to our board
Young Meagher of the sword;
'Tis he will sheathe that battle-axe in Saxon gore."

Needless to add that these were not adverted to. But the talk was of his success as a lecturer; of his discourses, which lasted full two years in delivery; of Australia; and of the ever-present "Irish Question." He afterwards became an officer in the North and South War. He met an untimely death by falling from the steamer's deck in the Upper Missouri, in the year 1867, and thus ended an eventful career.

One of the incidents which delighted his interlocutor was heard subsequently. Someone, in the presence of Meagher, spoke disrespectfully of Her Majesty the Queen, which so roused the anger of the rebel that, but for friendly interference, he would have given the unmannerly lout a sound thrashing !

The love of perpetual motion is seen not only in the cars, but in the very popular sport of sleighing, somewhat emulating that sense of rapid transit through streets. Throughout the Northern States the barometers fell in a day, and the bright balmy atmosphere gave way to cold weather about mid-January; and on three successive days—12th, 13th, and 14th—Broadway became alive with brisk sleighs of different sizes and shapes, after a good snowfall. The main features, however, were the huge sleigh-stages, or open cars on "runners," four rough-shod horses drawing them at good rattling speed to the tune of jingling bells, the conductor meanwhile going round on a projecting wooden cradle and collecting the fares. The sight is very pretty and exhilarating.

The intrepid smoker whiffs as if he were in a bar-room. There is a drawback, to which the newspapers direct attention, to this effect:—

"DANGEROUS SPORT.—Filling omnibus sleighs with big lumps of snow, ice, and street filth, and hurling them into other sleighs, knocking down men, women, and children, is shameful and dangerous. Some of the guilty parties were stage-conductors themselves."

The defenceless position of those being whisked along rapidly makes the usually permissible game

of snowballing indefensible here, as the essential
condition of being able to retaliate is impossible.
Few like target-practice if themselves the circle
aimed at. The old and feeble folk naturally retire
into private life on these occasions. Amongst them
was Washington Irving, who put off a journey for a
few days until, by the change of temperature, the

wayfarer ran no risks of being either pelted or assailed by rheums.

It was pleasant to witness the repression of these
escapades by those anxious to redress grievances. I
believe the press to be so in harmony with order
in the States that, attention being directed to
misdeeds, they were sure to receive the immediate
supervision of the police. These officials were attired
in coats of a light pepper colour, not attracting much
attention from the eye; but the grip was sufficient
when you looked at the limbs ensconced in them.

I went to see the Tombs prison, in Centre Street, then open to anyone on payment of a trifling consideration. Here is given its grim exterior elevation only. The inside is omitted, as I found it so terribly depressing to look at. Moreover, a reference to the description given in Dickens's "American Notes"

THE TOMBS PRISON

will be found all-sufficing. The identical negro seemed to have remained there as described by him, warming himself in the chill lower storey of the building. The watching warders, sitting on their iron-grated galleries, as they do at our Wormwood Scrubs prison, still sat there night and day, as I was

informed. A pervading mildewy smell, the result
of the low level of the foundations, was yet a feature

AN EXECUTION MORNING OUTSIDE THE TOMBS

of the place, from which you gladly escaped into the
fresher open air.

Grouped round the main building were seen stalls for apple-women, German grog-shops and lager-beer sellers, the latter resorted to by teamsters, who followed the example of Wordsworth's waggoner, and left their horses and their vehicles to linger driverless, whilst frowsy brats grinned at their own faces as seen distorted in the shiny panels of the vehicle.

Presently, whilst sketching, I noticed a curricle, which was pulled up at the prison-gate, disgorging a drunkard, who went and joined the roistering band of casuals I had seen inside in the yards awaiting the expiration of their few days of enforced sobriety. They are known as the " five days' men," the prison cicerone informed one.

On other occasions, though happily few, executions take place inside the prison yard. The expectant crowd outside consisted of loafers and people unable to obtain an entrance, owing to the crush for seats or standing-room.

I got into what is called a " Whitehall boat " with a stout sculler, who soon rowed me over the half-mile expanse of water dividing Governor's Island from the Battery, and thus I was enabled to see the dress of regulars—recruits in this instance—and their quarters in Fort Columbus. Few cared, it seems, to explore this stronghold, an exception being, I was

told, on the part of officials. General Pierce had
come over in this very skiff a few days before, so
the waterman averred; but whether with a view to
impress me with this adventitious importance, or
of enforcing extra payment in consequence, I was

GOVERNOR'S ISLAND

left in doubt. As I landed on the granite steps
leading up the bankside, my friend was told by the
sentinel to wait there till my return, an order which
evidently he received with an ill-grace, whilst a mere
Britisher was allowed to ramble about at large and to
sketch unmolested. Though not promising subjects
for the pencil, the few verandah-girt houses looked
as if the slightest mortar-practice would bring them
down with a run, and that the released supporting timbers might be helpfully utilized as floating
spars in a tide-way. This nocturnal mode of deser-
tion to the neighbouring Brooklyn shore was, it was

whispered, not at all an unusual event on the part of many finding a trimestrial practice of the goose-step over-irksome. The inside court resembled somewhat that of the four-cornered hotel yard, whilst outside of it the recruits were preparing for future vegetable growth by spreading manure over the fields. I got back to the boat, which deftly avoided innumerable lighters, ferry-boats, and pleasure yachts. I pacified the oarsman with a sufficient payment for my visit to this fortified post.

Although statistics show that during the Civil War over two millions of soldiers were then under arms (mostly volunteers, with the exception of fifty thousand regulars), comparatively few of these were to be seen parading or perambulating the streets in the fifties. Exceptionally, perhaps, might be seen a battalion returning from drill—smart and well set-up, with a business-like air. The rear was brought up by two negro files, one of whom carried the major's heavy spotted rug, and the other a wooden ensign on a pole. Between them was a diminutive unfledged recruit, over whose shoulders was slung the useful water canteen. Those I saw were called " Bow'ry Boys," or Democratic Guards.

Another band of volunteers, *i.e.*, the Fire Brigade, were at this time only the undeveloped raw material

for what has since then been made into a most efficient
and well-organised department. What was then a
motley band of a poorly disciplined though well-
meaning Salvage Corps, with only a number upon
their hats, and a speaking-trumpet in hand, as badges

VOLUNTEERS' MARCH

of their extemporised calling, have, I now understand, self-propelling steam-engines—going through the
streets at a smart trot—made by the Amoskeag Company, and burning houses are extinguished without
the excessive inundating deluges of former days,

making the calamity, it was said, from flooding far greater than that of the original fire.

Clinton Hall, with little architectural pretension as far as the exterior elevation was concerned—the house where the Mercantile Library carried on its useful

organisation—was in a street off Broadway, near the Astor House. It was the home, I believe, of the first Governor of New York, Sir Henry Clinton, and hence called Clinton Hall. The surplus funds accruing from the lectures are invested in books, thus gradually increasing the clerks' library. MSS. of interest, as

AFTER THE FIRE, NEW YORK

historical documents in the States, are also acquired and published; a savings bank being another sound feature.

New Year's Day is ushered in as a general holiday, the distinguishing feature being its devotion more especially to the satisfying of the young folks. Though Thackeray was in Boston, he commissioned me to distribute the proper amount of *bonbonnières*, which I did faithfully. As you are expected to call personally, and not vicariously, the task, though pleasing, becomes laborious if there be a large circle of acquaintanceship. It was a great relief at last to cease perambulating, and to sit down at the hospitable house of Mr. Pell.

7

The next day, January 2nd, I left New York for
Philadelphia, to arrange lecturing matters. The change
was bracing, and the scene was noble in its grand
simplicity, as the sun went down over Jersey City,
whilst I was crossing in the ferry from New York.
It was on a fine Sunday afternoon, and the red flare
brought out the line of roofs, topped—appropriately,
on the Sabbath—by its solitary steeple. I believe the
submarine tunnel is fast approaching completion here ;
a great convenience doubtless, but it will mulct
travellers of noble vistas in cloudland and of Venetian-
looking distances. Gone, too, will be the quaint

figure of the water-
seller, also a semi-
Venetian reminis-
cence, as this Creole
dealt out her
tumblers to the
thirsty on board in
the saloon. The
Maine liquor law,
in full force, for-
bade any more
exhilarating liquid
being dispensed to
quench thirst.
Solids also are sold.

CANVAS-BACK DUCKS

Here is a black trader (he was dressed, I recollect, in a deliciously toned pea-green coat) waiting for customers whilst sitting upon the central steps of the ferry crossing the Susquehanna. His specialty was

NEWS ROOM, PHILADELPHIA

the famous canvas-back duck, sold, as he announced, at one dollar and a quarter each. This favourite bird feeds upon the wild celery growing on islets about the bay, whence its world-famous flavour and delicacy.

The rest of our journey might have afforded matter for comment to those liking to ponder upon

the futility of making laws which cannot be enforced.
Here we were traversing tracts of country in which
penalties are supposed to be meted out rigorously to
those infringing sobriety ; yet, as a protest, you
heard endless cork-poppings, and occult topers might
be seen taking surreptitious bottles from their side-
pockets and applying them to their throats throughout their short travels.   These unruly spirits, becoming
confidential, took the surrounding company into their
consultations as to the best method of meeting the
coming Caudle lecturing of their spouses, which they
guessed would be of a lively kind, after having had
their fling at New York. The forecast seemed exhilarating to the company, which laughed consumedly
at the prospect in view. One non-abstainer seemed
sufficiently primed to receive any Caudle lecture with
equanimity.   I reached the cosy " Girard House "
quarters at Philadelphia, escaping with pleasure from
downpouring rain outside.

MEETING OF FRIENDS, PHILADELPHIA

CHAPTER III

Philadelphia—A Quakers' Meeting—Negro Disability—A Historical
  Porch—W. B. Read—Washington—Lecture on "Humour and
  Charity" at New York—Washington and Baltimore—Presidential
  Levée—The Ericsson—The Iron Jackson—Congress.

I soon, next morning, engaged a lecturing hall
from the stout good-humoured caretaker ; and after
due insertion of lecture announcements in the papers
and other matters therein-concerning, I rambled over
the town, which had a pleasant Quaker-like cleanliness
and stateliness, giving it a physiognomy of its own.

When one is tired of rambling, there is always the
pleasant reading-room resource. The *Ledger*, *National
Intelligencer*, and the *Union*, which are the names seen

upon the papers the two readers have been perusing
(p. 99), bring back to mind this admirable adjunct of
a newsroom, which is a feature of all American hotels.
They were salient Philadelphian organs of opinion,
doubtless exponents of the thoughts and feelings of
the Society of Friends, to which these twin figures
seemed also to belong.

Though Philadelphia had no statues at that time,
you soon gleaned that the three salient figures of its
history were—William Penn, its famed founder;
Benjamin Franklin; and, lastly, the wealthy Bordeaux
workman Girard, who had presented the town with
thirty millions of francs as a bequest.

William Penn is remembered and recalled by
endless popular announcements, to which his name is
attached.

Exemplifying this hero-worship, there was the
awning shading the hotel, embellished with his three-
cornered hat and wig; the hero holding his famous
treaty, which West's picture has made familiar.
Franklin's renowned hand-printing press is here.
Washington's chair—which you see put in his pictures,
but in which, characteristically, he is never seated—
is also religiously preserved in the museum.

Though a little out of order as to time, here may
be described fitly an incident connected with a stay
in Philadelphia.

Whilst sauntering along its main thoroughfare on a restful Sunday morning, I noticed a building, surrounded by gravelled spaces, walled in from the road, though the gateway lay invitingly open. The air of stillness and mystery about the place, and the traveller's scarce pardonable spirit of inquisitiveness, seemed to impel me to go in and solve my doubts.

I walked up steps to the inner door, which I opened, when I found myself looking from an elevated platform down on an assembled but mute congregation of men on one side and women on the other. This I, of course, saw at once was a Quakers' meeting. I closed the door, hoping I could reach a seat unnoticed, but every board of the floor creaked to my tread, and I was thankful when I was able to sit down, though

not a soul moved or turned round to see who the
intruder was, so enwrapped were they in their de-
votions. An elder, after an interval, got up and
addressed the people assembled, sat down after a
brief exordium, and without any apparent signal
everyone got up, and walked away and dispersed.
I afterwards made this a subject for a painting from
memory, and sent it to the Royal Academy.

More negro-limning engaged me as I left Philadelphia next day for Baltimore. It was not, as it
turned out, a cheerful incident which I was to carry
out, though begun without any idea further than that
of an ordinary
passenger's like-
ness. It happened
thus. On seeing a
good - humoured
negro attired in
a chimney-pot
hat, and leaning
upon his modest
linen bag (possi-
bly his whole be-
longings), the
sight was so novel
I sketched him;
but presently the

(Got into the wrong lot.)
Conductor:— How dare you nigga come & mix with white people!)
Exit Sambo & bundle in submissive silence to
the nigger-pew next the engine!
(At Philadelphia)   Feb 8ᵗʰ '53.

car-man came up with anger in his countenance, and beckoned him away, saying, " Get into the first car, sir—sitting here among white people, indeed ! " He moved away as told ; a mother clasping her infant, in an adjoining cushioned compartment, looked pity- ingly on the scene, as I did too. I now saw for the first time an ill-lighted compartment next the engine, in which were already ensconced a young negro and his wife, or female companion.

Whilst on this topic I may mention a pathetic story we were told at Baltimore of a lax white trader, who, besides his legitimate offspring, left a second family of dusky-coloured children. Not knowing, what was a fact, that he was insolvent, he left them free by his will. The creditors, not to be baulked, sold these little mulattoes as slaves, to be sent down South. Dire war has done this good—that such fell purposes can never more be carried out on a free soil.

After the tragic piece fitly comes the cheery inter- lude. As such may be here inserted the letter of invitation, running thus :—

"Baltimore, First M⁰., 22, 1853.

" E. CROWE.

"ESTEE⁰· FRIEND,—This will be handed thee by H. Stone, a mem- ber of our Lecture Committee. In case thee has not written A. C. Rhodes, Mr. Stone will bear to us any communication as regards time of commencing course, etc.—Respectfully,

" (Signed) ED⁰· M. NEEDLES."

In pursuance of the above I took up quarters at Barnum's comfortable hotel at Baltimore. Meeting the committee of the Mercantile Society, and the head of

BALTIMORE

the committee, Mr. Needles (a good name for a sharp treasurer), we, after little difficulty, arranged terms, settled the time of coming, etc., to mutual satisfaction.

The lectures were here to be given at the Universalist Church, and from the preacher's pulpit.

I give the appearance of the streets in the fifties. They had a good smack of old-world buildings at that time. The stepping-stones enabling the passer-by to avoid being wet-footed after continued rains, are as old as Pompeii as street-features and as contrivances saving shoe-leather. The square tower and flagstaff might have belonged to the contemporaries of the "Humorists." The trees also gave an antiquated flavour, though leafless at this time, as they spread bare stems before solidly built structures. Here I recollect noticing, dependent from a door-handle, a mournful piece of black drapery; this was a notice that there was a death

A NOTICE OF DEATH

in that house, and probably was a trans-Atlantic intimation substituted for the two mutes formerly standing in English doorways on these occasions.

On the return journey I met at the "Girard House" *table d'hôte* in Philadelphia an old familiar face, the handsome one of C. F. Henningsen. He was a sort of guerilla or free-lance, who had spent his life in camps, rather as a newspaper correspondent than himself under orders. He wrote, in 1832,

"Scenes from the Belgian Revolution." This was an opuscule in verse of threescore pages, which I purchased once on a bookstall—uncut, of course. He had after this been in the Carlist War of 1832 up to 1840, where he was near being shot, being captured by the Espartero party. He invited me to have a smoke in his rooms, which were full of different-patterned rifles and carbines, as if he already scented in the air the war between North and South. I heard that he took a commission under Walker the Filibuster, and became a general in the Confederate army in subsequent years. I introduced him to Thackeray, who was much struck with his presence, as a type of the free-lance not unworkable into romance. Charles Gruneisen, the able musical critic of after-years, was his companion in captivity in Spain, and narrowly escaped the short shrift given in those days to men of either side when captured. I believe "Little Moore," whose *nom de plume* was "Poco-Mas," the *Morning Chronicle* correspondent, was the chief means of getting both of them off, owing to his interceding in their favour with Espartero, the commander of the army, and the British legion under General Evans.

On the 18th of January, before leaving Philadelphia, I sketched the somewhat squat proportions of the classical Portico, in front of which was read

the "Declaration of Independence." Here it is reproduced, as is also often the facsimile of that
document itself. The events of the period to which
it relates were often matter of discussion between

THE DECLARATION OF INDEPENDENCE

Thackeray and his friend Mr. T. B. Reed, the
able diplomatist, whose genial hospitality made our
sojourn so pleasant in that city. All readers of
Thackerayan sayings and doings must ever refer
back to his kindly written, though brief, sentences.

about the author in his tribute to him called "Haud Immemor." It is a pity, however, that the two visits—that of 1853 and 1855—are sometimes insufficiently defined, and rather jumbled together.

On the next day (19th) we shifted our camp, and, changing cars at Baltimore, went on to Washington. The change was not a beneficial one, as we got into a luggage train—a necessity arising from the fact that the train meant for us had been run into by a "burden train," which we supposed to be American for "goods."

Thackeray has himself put on record the originating source of his lecture on "Charity and Humour," about this time, when we returned once more to New York. Some friends wished to benefit a "Ladies' Society for the Employment and Relief of the Poor," and he volunteered to write a new discourse to be delivered for that purpose.

He took a whole day for the task, lying down in his favourite recumbent position in bed, smoking, whilst dictating fluently the phrases as they came. I took them down, with little or no intermission from breakfast-time till late in the dusk of the evening. The dinner-gong sounded, and the manuscript was then completed. I remember his pleased exclamation at this *tour de force*—not usual with him—" I don't

know where it's all coming from !" In many instances Boileau's distich came to mind, when the composition was rebellious—

> " Tel mot, pour avoir réjoui le lecteur,
> A coûté bien souvent des larmes à l'auteur "—

but in this case it was not so; the phrasing of
the words as they are read, flows with the easy
charm of their production. The charge of self-repe-
tition, made heedlessly against it, was scarcely avoid-
able in the first part, which is a recapitulation of the
" Humorists' " drift of purpose. These eighteenth-
century wits are passed in review in the first half,
as a foil to their subsequent comparison with the
modern forms of " Humour " and " Charity " to be
found in the works of contemporaries, and to whom a
noble tribute of respectful admiration is paid so
touchingly. Doubtless the incentive of a benevolent
motive was inspiriting to the author.

The lecture was first given a day or two after, on
the 31st of January, at the Church of the Messiah,
in Broadway, at three o'clock in the afternoon. The
charge for each ticket was one dollar, and the net
result was about twelve hundred dollars. The ladies
expressed their gratification at this windfall.

When we reached Washington we found it in
what is known as a whirl of " high jinks," owing to

the interminable succession of balls, concerts, parties, and banquets, to which Thackeray, and through him myself, were hospitably invited. Lecturing had to lie in abeyance till Lenten time allowed this less mundane form of amusement to be indulged in.

It would require a graphic pen to enumerate these hospitalities, foremost amongst which were those given by Sir Philip (then plain Mr.) Crampton at the British Embassy. The ladies were as much struck by the yellow plush liveries of our representative as was Nathaniel Hawthorne, as he informs us, about this time, when dining with the Mayor of Liverpool, or at the London Reform Club.

Senator Hamilton Fish also entertained sumptuously. The conversation, I remember, took an etymological turn. Washington Irving was asked the origin of "wilt" as a word, which he professed not to know, the Dutch derivation of "withering" not being apparently in his spirits or in his vocabulary. Senator Seward asked Thackeray how his own name would be pronounced in England, to which the reply was, "Like sewer—I think," an unsavoury idiom, which did not meet with his approbation.

Another senator, Mr. G. T. Davis, welcomed us to his friendly table, his son being an old friend of the guest of the evening, as secretary of the American Minister in London.

To sum up these *symposia*, the effect was to make the off-evenings of the lecturer, spent at Baltimore at the Universalist Church, quite a relief to him. He liked ascending to the pulpit there; delivered his lay sermon, and returned to sleep at our Washington lodging. The modest appliances there pleased him by way of contrast. In the morning the black servant used to bring in the teapot in her hand whilst smoking her pipe, which, when her tobacco was spent, she used to deposit upon my bedroom

A BLACK SERVANT

stove, and so perfume it with its aroma all day. A young mulatto helped her who had quite artistic proclivities. He used, uninvited, to take up my sketches, and pass very apposite critical remarks in a good-natured way.

February 18*th.*—On one of the evenings when I

8

was left in solitary possession of this lodging, I thought it would be fulfilling a pleasing duty to present my respects to President Fillmore, then giving farewell receptions at the White House, like those of the Speaker of the English House of Commons, called

Gen' Washington
White House.

Levées, held late in the evenings. Not knowing the exact costume one was expected to don on the occasion, I recollect making the inquiry of an intelligent storekeeper from whom I was making a purchase. In a *nonchalant* manner he said that the crush was so great on these occasions that no one thought of going there in any dress but the very oldest suit in their

wardrobe; "in fact, the worse the better." It is
needless to add that, easily seeing through his desire
to take "a rise out of the Britisher," I put on my
best suit of black, and appeared at the appointed
hour. Here is a sketch of the scene, done from

A PRESIDENTIAL RECEPTION

recollection. By the Head of the State stood a gentle-
man-usher, who came forward and inquired your name;
the President shook hands, with a pleasant " I'm glad
to see you," and you passed on, as did hundreds of
others—in couples for the most part. The queer note
of the evening was to see a stalwart son of toil, who
seemed unconsciously to have followed out to the
letter my friend the counter-jumper's injunction, and

had made his appearance in the frowsy garb of a prairie labourer. He held a dirty misshapen cap in his hand, his boots were dusty and worn, and near him was his son, probably weary, leaning his soiled garments against the white-and-gold papered walls, and possibly leaving there the marked outline of his presence. People laughed as if at a good joke, and passed on, whilst the staring "hawbuck" stood riveted by the scene of splendour. French marquis, foreign diplomats, citizens from all parts, elbowed each other in the throng. G. Stuart's portrait of General Washington was on the walls. The laurelled bust of the hero was on a recess over the doorway, both seemingly looking down blandly on the scene before them.

By an invariable courteous pre-arrangement, every four years the outgoing President accompanies the in-coming one for a while, in order, as it were, that the latter may be amicably introduced, and witness the public functions of Washington. Thus both President Fillmore and President Pierce honoured Thackeray by going together to hear his lecture at Carusi's Rooms. He compared them, to their amusement, to " the two Kings of Brentford smelling at one rose."

On another occasion they, as we also did, joined an invited party of guests to witness the mechanism of the new caloric ship recently completed by John

Ericsson. The cost of the vessel and her fittings had, it was said, amounted to 130,000 dollars. She was

PRESIDENTS PIERCE AND FILLMORE

moored in the stream, and as she was seen high above water-mark, looked at this early date capsizable. The two Presidents, discussing her probable future,

which was trumpeted as "promoting a new era in
naval propulsion," are here grouped together, as they
stood apart waiting for the tender which was to fetch

General Cass in the Senate

GENERAL CASS

the assembled company on board her. There was an
amusing instance given, as we got on board, of the difficulties that superior frames, mental and bodily, have
to encounter in adapting themselves to the situation.
The breeze of the riverside had chilled most people,

who at once took refuge below deck. I noticed the small form of Washington Irving, as seen through the intervening steps of the companion ladder, beneath which he was ensconced; whilst Thackeray had, in order to chat with him, carefully to keep his head

THE SUPREME COURT IN SESSION

between the roof-beams, as otherwise there was insufficient height to enable him to keep his head erect or to stand straight on his legs. The vessel might be, as she was stated to be, 260 feet in length, but altitudes barely corresponded with the human measurements.

Though many eloquent masters of speech from

Congress were of the party, few or no discourses were
delivered after the sumptuous lunch set out—due, no
doubt, to sympathetic respect for the feelings of the
President, General Pierce. He had lost his only son,
aged thirteen, and his wife had been injured in a railway accident only two months before the event here
recorded. The engines alone kept up voluble snorts
now and then. It is grievous to relate that this result
of twenty years of thought and labour and expense
foundered a year or so afterwards in a tornado off
Sandy Hook, the port-holes being open.

Before our arrival at Washington the newspapers
had announced in leaded type:—

"THE IRON JACKSON.

"Congress adjourned on Saturday, 8th January, and went under
the belly of the new iron horse and rider just erected in Washington
to the memory of General Jackson. Hero-worship pays."

Subsequently this bronze equestrian monument was
unveiled with demonstrations of its national importance. It was during a saunter, whilst passing through
Lafayette Square, that Thackeray saw it. He happened to let out, at a private house, his opinion of the
merits of the statue, which were thus summed up:—
"The hero was sitting in an impossible attitude, on
an impossible horse with an impossible tail." This
criticism was good-naturedly repeated, and was then

made the subject of an attack upon the objector in an obscure paper. He was bluntly informed that "the prejudices of English people were incorrigible," etc. etc. The sculptor had never seen any equestrian statue, and it was therefore excusable to fail in such a gigantic task. The fault was that of mistaken laudations on the part of others. The most sensible and competent judges—Charles Sumner amongst the rest—joined in the obloquy which seems to appertain to too many sculptural equestrian efforts, at home and abroad.

When invited afterwards to visit General Scott, at the War Department, he showed us, hung up on the walls, a trophy of the siege of New Orleans, of which General Jackson was the hero. It was the sword of Pulaski, who fell on that day. He liked to dwell upon warlike deeds, in which he had been conspicuously successful, in preference to Presidential campaigning, in which, though beaten, he bore his defeat manfully, as his leonine face would lead one to expect he would do. Here is its outline.

GENERAL SCOTT

Senator Sumner conducted us over the whole of

the different sections of Congress, beginning with a
view of the central Rotunda, embellished with life-
size illustrations of the War of Independence,
executed by Trumbull. This painter, a pupil of
Benjamin West in England, had closely followed
General Washington as his *aide-de-camp*, and was
therefore an intelligent witness of many scenes
he depicted; hence their value in costume and in
portraiture. Thackeray, with his trained critical eye,
pronounced them admirably good; and so they are.
I never cease to regret having lost an elaborate
sketch I made of the House of Representatives in
session; it was sent, by Thackeray's advice, to an
illustrated paper, and was not published, and never
recovered by me; else these pages would have contained likenesses of the President's chair topped by
the huge eagle, and the semicircular seats thronged
by members at their desks, the Hon. Mr. Marshall
ably arguing for an increase of their naval force,
the proposition scouted by irascible opponents, spring-
ing on their legs. I have, however, replaced this by
a few stray bits—as taken from the Strangers' Gallery
—of Senators, such as the portrait of the venerable
Anglophobist, General Cass, whose locks were as hale as
his oratory was vigorous, and the sketch of the "Supreme Court" in session, held in what used to be in
former days the Senate Chamber, much smaller than its

successor, the Ionic columns of Potomac marble, as
ponderous as the judgments seem to be to the un-
initiated listeners, whose numbers are few. Neither is
the Law Library, which lies underneath it, thronged

A STUMP

with readers ; quite unheeded are the folios, which, I
suppose, are only for fitful legal researches after pre-
cedents.

It was quite a relief to emerge into the open air,
and to watch, mayhap, one of the numerous processions

passing by, headed by their blatant brass-band instru-
ments. A turn of the road brought me before a square
wooden structure in the open air, which I sketched.
It was meant for oratorical displays, and is known as a
" stump "—quite a national institution.

Somewhat footsore with so much lionising, we were
glad to find good restoratives at the National Restau-
rant. The waiter alone was refreshing to look at as he
brought in some dainty, which, at this distance of time,
as depicted here, looks insufficient to satisfy three
hungry mortals, as we were.

CHAPTER IV

AFTER a three weeks' stay at Washington, we left
it at night, always a dreary time of exit. It was
necessary to do so to catch the steamer which was to
waft us down the Potomac. There were plenty of
fine Rembrandtesque night-effects to be noted. Amid
the general bustle, and in the motley groups hurry-
ing on board, you could dimly see the man at the
tiller, in a small cabin amidships. The idea—at first
entertained—of sleeping on board proved illusory.
A lusty negro rang the bell announcing supper, con-
sisting of oyster soup. Another deck-hand invited
" gentlemen to take de tickets "—clapper going again;
then another summons to have luggage labelled. Someone stated we were near the " Dismal Swamp ; " this
seemed to chime in with our lowered spirits, deafened
as we were by tintinabulary sounds.

With dawn these revived, and the sun lifted the
misty veil. The eyes, jaded by the somewhat bleak
scenery of Washington and its neighbourhood at this

season of the year, were refreshed by vistas of green
leafage.   I sketched the distant outline of Washington's
home, Mount Vernon.   We tried to spot the "New
Castlewood," which was raised on the beautiful banks
of the Potomac.   The delightful season alluded to in
the same passage, called the Indian summer, though
belonging to late autumn, seemed to have its counter-
part in March, for the heat of the day was considerable
as we neared Richmond, after changing from steamboat
into cars once more.

We came into Richmond, as it were, on the day
after the fair ; some hitch in the communication had
caused a day's delay.   The hall at Richmond was
crammed with an expectant audience, who had to be
politely informed that the lecture was postponed till
the next evening.   They took it in good part when
informed of the unlucky missing of the train, and
dispersed after receiving a telegraphic apology.

As if it were but yesterday, the trite incidents of
travel crop up at times in the memory.   Thus I
remember, at a station between Fredericksburg and
Richmond, which was on a steepish gradient, two
stalwart negroes arresting the train's movement down-
wards by periodical thrusts of wooden logs, giving
the cars and ourselves quite pleasing jerks in the
process, treating these vehicles as a waggoner does
his team on going downhill.   (There were no brakes

TESTING TOBACCO, VIRGINIA

here in these days.) We were glad to reach our final destination, Richmond, and to enter its comfortable hotel. The next day's paper was somewhat mixed in its announcements of fashionable arrivals, thus: " Mr. Thackeray, the celebrated author; Mr. Anderson, Wizard of the North;" to which, as far as I recollect, were added some species of prodigy and a wild buffalo. If one was inclined to wince, at first, at this not quite dignified medley of caterers for public amusement, the feeling soon wore off into one of positive liking for the unpretending and cheerful conversation of the conjurer. He was surrounded by quite a troup of young wizards, who all helped him in his sleight of hand and evolutions. The black waiters wore stiff white bows round their necks, and appeared in black coat-tails, and plied the company with all the delicacies, including the luscious banana, much relished in its fresh state. This feasting on the ordinary fare was many times relieved by the unceasing kindliness of some of the notables, who threw open their hearts and their homes to the welcome personator of English literature, not excluding self for the nonce. The English intonation was heard once more, owing to the traditional British schooling still kept up in those days in Virginia.

This State, as all know, is especially endeared to the British tar by furnishing him with the toothsome "quid"—with which he has ever been plentifully regaled from the fields of the district, at the rate of about 130 dollars profit per acre. The tobacco-leaf fluctuates some-what in quality. In my peregrina-tions through the business part of the town I came across the scene depicted on p. 127. The experts of the trade were to be seen grasp-ing in their arms several of the choicest speci-mens of the brands, whilst muscular negroes, armed with crow-bars, lifted each of the compressed

RICHMOND

parcels, so as to test them at the central portions. The mass of these emitted a pleasant honey-dew smell, and evolved mental calculations as to the prodi-gious amount of mastication ensuing. This, however,

9

if I could trust a voluntary informant afterwards, was not, after all, so vast as imagined. He said, "But for the income it brings in, we could easily chew the whole Virginia plant ourselves." No wonder, then, is it to see the capacious hotel expectorators generally festooned with the ejected, well-moistened leafage. Hitched on one of the rafters of the room was noticeable a trophy of the late Presidential campaign, in the shape of a small picture of the favourite candidate mounted upon a prancing charger; this was fastened to a pole, and bore the inscription— "In General Pierce we put a manly trust." It was paraded thus at the hustings as a party emblem, and their man had won the day.

The departing trains for the South cross the brawling rocky bed of the James river by a wooden bridge. Here it is, overleaf, in the immediate foreground of the sketch; beyond, is given the general aspect of Richmond, with its houses capped by the classic-shaped Capitol as it looked forty years ago, a fair notion of its aspect at that period. Somehow these rough-looking storehouses and unpretending tenements are always more pleasing to the artistic sense than are the stately fabrics of more modern-looking towns. The handsome verdure-surrounded villas are here out of sight.

The 3rd of March, 1853, is a date well imprinted on

my memory. I was sitting at an early *table d'hôte* breakfast by myself, reading the ably conducted local newspaper, of which our kind friend was the editor. It was not, however, the leaders or politics which attracted my eye, so much as the advertisement columns, containing the announcements of slave sales, some of which were to take place that morning in Wall Street, close at hand, at eleven o'clock.

Ideas of a possibly dramatic subject for pictorial illustration flitted across my mind ; so, with small notepaper and pencil, I went thither, inquiring my way to the auction rooms. They consisted, I soon discovered, of low rooms, roughly white-washed, with worn and dirty flooring, open, as to doors and windows, to the street, which they lined in succession. The buyers clustered first in one dealer's premises, then moved on in a body to the next store, till the whole of the tenants of these separate apartments were disposed of. The sale was announced by hanging out a small red flag on a pole from the doorway. On each of these was pinned a manuscript notice of the lot to be sold. Thus I read :—" Fifteen likely negroes to be disposed of between half-past nine and twelve—five men, six women, two boys, and two girls." Then followed the dealer's signature, which corresponded to that inscribed over the doorway. When I got

E.J.C. Richmond Virginia - March 3rd 53.   Slaves waiting to be sold

IN THE RICHMOND SLAVE MARKET

into the room I noticed, hanging on the wall, a
quaintly framed and dirty lithograph, representing
two horsemen galloping upon sorry nags, one of
the latter casting its shoe, and his companion having
a bandaged greasy fetlock; the marginal inscription
on the border was to this effect:—" Beware of what
you are about." I have often thought since how
foolish it was, on my part, not to have obeyed
this premonitory injunction to act prudently in such
a place as this was. The ordeal gone through by
the several negroes began by making a stalwart
hand pace up and down the compartment, as would

be done with a horse, to note his action. This proving satisfactory, some doubt was expressed as to his ocular soundness. This was met by one gentleman unceremoniously fixing one of his thumbs into the socket of the supposed valid eye, holding up a hair by his other hand, and asking the negro to state what was the object held up before him. He was evidently nonplussed, and in pain at the operation, and he went down in the bidding at once. More hands were put up; but by this time feeling a wish for fresh air, I walked out, passing intervening stores and the grouped expectant negroes there.

I got to the last and largest end store, and thinking the sales would occupy a certain time, I thought it might be possible to sketch some of the picturesque figures awaiting their turn. I did so. On rough benches were sitting, huddled close together, neatly dressed in grey, young negro girls with white collars fastened by scarlet bows, and in white aprons. The form of a woman clasping her infant, ever touching, seemed the more so here. There was a muscular field-labourer sitting apart; a rusty old stove filled up another space. Having rapidly sketched these features, I had not time to put my outline away before the whole group of buyers and dealers were in the compartment. I thought the best plan was to go on unconcernedly; but, perceiving me so engaged, no one would bid. The auctioneer, who had mounted his table, came down and asked me whether, "if I had a business store, and someone came in and interrupted my trading, I should like it." This was unanswerable; I got up with the intention of leaving quietly, but, feeling this would savour of flight, I turned round to the now evidently angry crowd of dealers, and said, "You may turn me away, but I can recollect all I have seen." I lingered in a neighbouring vacated store, to give myself the attitude of leisurely retreat, and I left this stifling atmosphere of human traffic. "Crowe has been very imprudent," Thackeray wrote to a friend afterwards. And, in truth, I soon reflected it was so. It might have led to unpleasant results to the lecturer himself, bound, as he went South, not to be embroiled in any untoward accident involving interference with the question of slavery, then at fever-heat, owing to Mrs. Stowe's fiery denunciations in "Uncle Tom's Cabin." Though I have no real ground for the assumption, it has often occurred to me that the incident was allowed to drop quietly, owing to the timely intervention of friends, who threw oil upon these troubled waters, and buried their wrath in oblivion.

The narrative here given is so simple as to bear the stamp of truth which needs no further corroboration.

Still, by way of amplification of scenes subsequent to my withdrawal—or flight, if the reader prefers, though I was not sensible of it—I herewith give the account, which I found published exactly a week after in the *New York Daily Tribune* of March 10th, written by someone who, unknown to myself, was present on this occasion :—

Extract of part of a letter in the *New York Daily Tribune* of March 10th, 1853, written by a New Yorker on Southern tour. The letter is dated " Richmond, Va., Thursday, March 3rd, 1853 : "—

A SLAVE AUCTION IN VIRGINIA

[After describing the previous sales, he comes to the last one.]

" A scene occurred in this room which ' may yet be heard from.' Just before the sale commenced, a young well-dressed gentleman entered the room—placing himself in one corner of the room— began to take a sketch, and had proceeded quite far before he was noticed by anyone but myself. At last he attracted the attention of some of the bystanders, until full twenty or more were looking over his shoulder. They all seemed pleased with what he was doing, so long as the sketch was a mere outline, but as he began to finish up the picture, and form his groups of figures, they began to see what he was about, and then someone went up privately to the auctioneer (who had by this time got one or two sold), and informed him what the man was doing. He came down from the stand, went and overlooked what he was doing for a moment, and saw himself written down for the first time in his life. He inquired of the man what he was doing. The answer was, ' I do not know that I am bound to answer your inquiry.' Mr.

Auctioneer took his stand again, but was evidently so enraged that he could not go on, for by this time the whole company was aware of what was being done. And some proclaimed with a *loud oath* that the likeness was 'd——d fine,' 'most splendid;' others were for 'footing' him. The artist took the hint, however, without the kick, and left the room. But now we had a specimen of Southern *bravery*. They were all sure that he was an Abolitionist, and they all wanted to 'lend a foot' to kick him, while one small gentleman said he would pay twenty-five dollars to hire a negro to do it. The excitement soon passed over; not, however, without leaving on my mind the truth of the maxim that 'He who fights and runs away, may live to fight another day.'"

After these sales we saw the usual exodus of negro slaves, marched under escort of their new owners across the town to the railway station, where they took places, and "went South." They held scanty bundles of clothing, their only possession. These were the scenes which in a very short number of years made one realise the sources of the fiercest of civil wars, and which had their climax when General Grant mustered his forces upon this spot as a centre against the equally gallant General Lee. Placid enough at the time I speak of were the avocations of this place, which is built on a slope, as is its English namesake. Towering above the rest of the houses was the Capitol, inside which was an antiquated stove, which had done service ever so long ago. All genuine works of art stamp a place as quite out of the common.

The State House at Richmond so excels, and Houdon's statue of General Washington stands there as a great masterpiece. The story is pleasantly told on the occasion of the famous French sculptor's visit to

Old Stove at Richmond. Virginia

Mount Vernon. So scrupulous were these great craftsmen they disdained heroics, but they gave alike the exact measurement of the stature, the simple pose, the serene smile, and the imperishable marble form of those before them. One wonders why these

noble versions are not simply reproduced, instead of
modern caracoling equestrian statues filling squares,
which give no mortal any pleasure to look at.   The
clean-shaven face of the " Father of his Country " has

AFTER HOUDON'S WASHINGTON *

doubtless had the effect of giving encouragement to
all good Americans—his children—to do likewise.

   Exemplifying this, here is the quaint posture of
nearly horizontal rest in which the barber plies the
razor upon the cheeks and chins of most of his
customers, that curious excrescence — the goatee —

* Inscribed thus : " Fait par Houdon, citoyen Français, 1788."

E. CYONE.

AN AMERICAN BARBER'S, RICHMOND, VA.

betwixt lip and chin, forming the exception to the usually clean-shaven face.

Petersburg (Virginia) sharing with Richmond in strategic importance during the Civil War, and since that adding its record of valorous defence, was at this time a somewhat somnolent-looking town. I went thither, and made all due arrangements for lecturing. I recollect carrying off in triumph from a drug store a high desk enamelled in white, the MS. leaves of the lecture needing this kind of support, generally dispensed with by extempore speakers. The walls were placarded with announcements of the discourse ; the papers were full of advertisements that the lecture would take place.

Thackeray came down by an afternoon train. On inquiry at the ticket offices it was found that very few seats had been taken ; the advertisements in the papers had remained unheeded for the most part. As the evening was warm, the hall windows were left open ; and as I took a seat on a bench in a square below, I could hear the well-known sentences as they fell from the lecturer's lips, and issued, over well-nigh empty benches, into the calm air of the outside square, where, lounging sadly, I heard them. We philosophised over this queer breach in the hitherto continuous spell of successes, as he afterwards whiffed his cigar, without anyone joining us, in the hotel parlour.

In the early morning I felt myself seeking relief from enforced mutism by button-holing a negro whom I watched digging in a small field. To my query he replied he was working upon an allotment-plot, many of his fellows having the same small ownership of the soil for small market produce given them by liberal landlords. We took the very earliest train to Richmond, glad to get once more amongst friends and to cheerful converse. The sketch of Petersburg presented overleaf (a view which is a little way from the street pavements) gives a notion of the place, at that time quite innocent of forts—unconscious of coming warfare, and that they would bear the brunt of a good deal of it hereafter.

The Easter Monday holiday was here kept, as with us, by popular *dolce far niente* rambles and quiet enjoyment of all factory and other hands, clad in their best.

I sketched one of the factories on the banks of the Appomattox, to which a bare tree was the picturesque foreground. I had time only to indicate the sand collectors and their carts in the front of it.

The night-travelling in the cars in the South, as usual, only admits of snatches of broken rest. You doze perhaps, and you are aroused by the negro fireman, who comes and rakes out the cinders choking

up the stove-grate, and playfully sending a considerable part of the ashes flying into the air you breathe.
He, however, relieved your sensations of being
parched, by then bringing a large bucket full of
water and a huge wooden long-handled ladle. All

EASTER MONDAY, PETERSBURG, VA.

who are clustered for warmth round the stove, and
who had stretched out grimy stockinged toes
towards this centre, refresh themselves, turn round,
and become somnolent once more. There is a fine
democratic air of simplicity about the whole arrangement. As dawn comes, you are rewarded by seeing

E. Crowe.

ON THE BANKS OF THE APPOMATTOX, PETERSBURG, VA.

through the many-paned windows of the car—which, in fact, are on all sides of it—by witnessing the roseate rays of the rising sun illuminating the pine forests, superbly decked out in rime. You are inclined on these occasions to side with the humoristic views of Mr. Rudyard Kipling's latest doctrine, and to pro-

ON BOARD THE "GOVERNOR DUDLEY"

nounce these magical fleeting effects as transcending more enduring canvas-smearings in interest. The calm Sunday's rest came as we settled at the journey's end at Wilmington, North Carolina. The devout congregation of negroes in the gallery of the church there dwells in the mind long after the sermon and its text have been forgotten. Their cheerful faces were a homily.

The next day we took tickets in the small steamer plying between Wilmington and Charleston. The dolphins were rolling over in the shallow waters in aquatic somersaults. Our captain, trumpet in hand, looked so rotund, you felt that, if thrown overboard by ill-fate, he also would have rotated. He, however, did his business of steering us at the rate of seventeen knots an hour steadily over the billows. Skilfully threading his way through shoals and shallows, passing sea-girt forts of the old war pattern—so soon to be replaced by newer ones, and to hoist the Con-

Charleston. march 7.ᵗʰ ʼ5ᵗʰ

GUARD

federate standard in gallant defence—we got safely into Charleston harbour, and found rooms in the huge "Charleston Hotel."

A time-worn copy of the *Charleston Daily Courier*, dated Tuesday morning, March 8th, 1853, is before me as I write these lines. It contains this announcement : — " Passengers yesterday (7th) arrived per steamer *Governor Dudley* from Wilmington, North Carolina." Here follow the names, " Thackery " (*sic*),

10

" Crowe," coming at the close. The faulty spelling is, however, amended in the small leader announcing the arrival at " Charleston Hotel," which adds :— " This evening, at the Hibernian Hall, at 7.30, he will begin a course of three lectures, viz., on Tuesday (8th), Thursday (10th), and Friday (11th) ; tickets for the course, 1 dollar ; single lecture, 50 cents." These were, of course, highly relished by the *élite* of Charleston. They gave full vent to their well-known hospitalities, and much lionising was the result. Thackeray made here several drawings with his gold nib, some of which have been published and facsimiled by the wonderful new processes. Borrowing of him the same invaluably pointed pen, I made a few sketches in this city. First is the " Réveille ! " sounded by fife and drum, calling out the negroes, secluded within doors during the darkness of night, and issuing at this call to the factories in the early morning. The rousing summons reverberated round the Guard House, plentifully decorated with manual shackles at the time I speak of, some of which we were allowed to handle on the previous night over a pleasant palaver with the captain in command. This rule of nocturnal retirement was obviously relaxed whenever a negro ball was given. We had the privilege of being invited to see one of these amusements. The saltatory features of

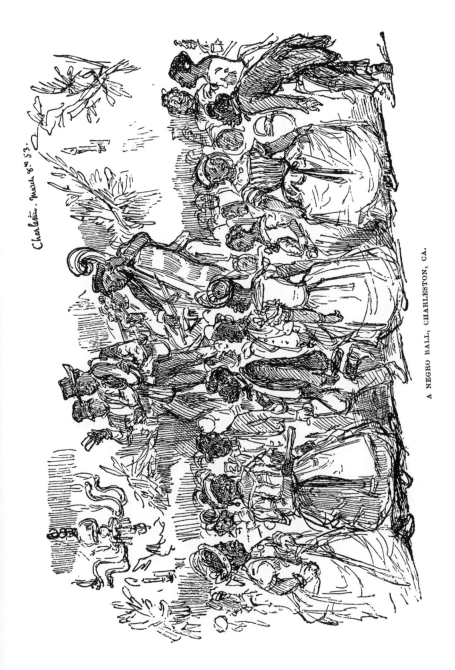

Charleston. March 8th 53.

A NEGRO BALL, CHARLESTON, CA.

the scene here given were quaint yet picturesque.
The minstrels were embowered in greenery as they
played waltzes and quadrilles, which were danced
with great zest, and the hall rang with good-humoured
laughter. The refreshments were limited to spruce-
beer, of which we drank thankfully, as administering
a novel sensation to the jaded palate. The striking
features of negro evening dress consisted in astonish-

ing turbans with marabou feathers, into
which odd accessories of squib shape
and other forms were inserted, which
gave the ladies the appearance of going
off, but not in the sense usually attached by chaperons to the term. We
went home in high humour. Truth
compels me to state that if a prize
had to be awarded for expectorators,
Charleston, at this time, would have
carried off the palm. The spectacle
has been, however, depicted on a
previous page.

More exhilarating groups call for notice. The
entrance hall of the hotel presents rather an ani-
mated scene, Charleston being the rendezvous of
several lines of communication from New York,
Havannah, or elsewhere. The piles of trunks form
perfect barricades, which can be contemplated from

AT THE CHARLESTON HOTEL

the convenient lounging-benches on all sides by -the numerous smokers there assembled.

I asked a young negress to come and have her likeness taken at the hotel, and she did so. She was a pea-nut seller, was quite modest and re- tiring, but she confided to us her great grievance against one of the known ordinances of slavery. She wished to go and see a play, but was not allowed the privilege at that time. A friend came in, to whom I showed the sketch, who cor- roborated her statement. I suppose this disability has since been rescinded, and has ceased to be an order enforced.

Amongst the pleasant remembrances of this time was that of meeting Professor Agassiz, who was then lecturing upon such subjects as Cryptogamous Plants, and Scientific Surveys of Pine and Fir Species. It is terrible to think that the instructive discourse of such a master of science falls on the non-scientific mind with no responsive chord, from sheer incom- petence to assimilate the abstruse matters under discussion.

Passing now from gay science to dull fact, the scene of the Charleston slave auction is here given, as a contrast to the Richmond version. Here it was in the open air, and by its picturesque elements lost many of its dismal features. The hands to be disposed

PETER "*Misho.*" "*CHUBBS*" & ABRAHAM   Henry *Douglass*
Charleston. March 12ᵗʰ 5's   of *obtain ill.*

of were fine strapping sons of toil. There were
ninety of them, all coming from an estate which was
being sold off. They had been employed in the
rice-fields of the Combahee river, flowing past the
Beaufort and Colleton districts towards the Atlantic.
I was much attracted by the group of women,
especially by a stout matron clasping her infant in
her arms, to whose points the dealer pointed with
emphasising forefinger. On the right hand was to
be seen the emblematic tree of the State, the graceful palmetto, protected by a square bar-grating. Further away was an earth-imbedded howitzer, acting as
prop to the lounger. Throw in the old Exchange
walls as a background, the tall masts of the cotton-
laden liners in the far distance, and the not inhar-
monious dresses of the slaves, and you have a picture,
painful it is true, but also quite curious, as a record
of bygone slavery times, actually reproduced as it was,
and not the result of imaginary composition.

Leaving these throngs of labour for those of
fashion, here is a sketch of one of the principal streets
of Charleston, the chief feature of it being St.
Michael's Church, built in the middle of the last
century by a pupil of Wren's. This gives it quite
an old English air, also consonant with other linger-
ing Old World traditions yet found here, such as
often sending children to be educated in Europe, as
was done by their forefathers.

But for the change in the lady's attire as to her
bonnet, as you see her issuing from the stationer's
shop, attended by a negro servant, and ready to step
upon the semicircular stone into her carriage, the
whole scene reminds one of the old prints of our
squares (where some of these stepping-stones still
survive) a hundred years ago.

On the Charleston Quays the negro population
affords opportunities for the pencil in their physiognomy, their dresses, and their callings. Look, for
example, at the youth, with brush in hand, dipping
it into a tar-pot, in order to mark the proper hiero-
glyphics upon the side of the compressed cotton bale.
There he sits enthroned—not a bad emblem of the
saying "Cotton is king." Other boys, whose faces
reveal varying coloured parentage, please by a sort of
general good-humoured intelligence. You trace these,
and also types of stalwart men marked by the same

THE CHARLESTON SLAVE MARKET

characteristics. To these may be joined the tripartite
sketch of "Little Rebecca," though hailing from

ST. MICHAEL'S CHURCH, CHARLESTON

another community, yet of kindred race, and beam-
ing with a sort of self-contentment always pleasant
to witness.

Little Rebecca   Richmond March 31-53

Joseph

Peter goes to confirstain in the gun
Doesn't know hirago as he came from his country as your boy
his wife is out during working & cooking
Gets 4 dollars a month & keep.

Charleston March 24th 53.

Oncalla will have asked slightly easy
to on de deck olde time
he didn't hear nothin.

Wharf-Hand

Farther away, when leaving haunts of the hard toilers, you notice market women awaiting the chance customers for their sweet potatoes, luscious bananas, and other products of that generous soil, till tired, and passing labyrinths of tiled houses, you get back to rest at the caravansary.

The balmy April atmosphere had brought with it the freshly imported spring *toilettes* from Paris, had enhanced the famed complexions of the feminine portion of the community, and had enticed them abroad to air both under the protecting parasols which they carried about with them in Broadway, or in the Carolinian lounge of King Street,

Charleston March 26

or beneath the ampler shop-awnings, screening the already fierce sun's rays. In church pews, too, the winsome faces were also noticeable, and later on at the dining-rooms of the Clarendon Hotel. The building, topped by the two "Stars and Stripes" flagstaffs, seen in the Broadway sketch (on p. 163), is the then newly opened Metropolitan Hotel of brown stone.

" COTTON IS KING "

American hotels are generally well placarded with warning notices enjoining visitors to be on their guard against the depredations of the thieves frequenting them in search of their prey, also an Old World institution. A young English Engineer officer, Rankin by name, a distant relative of Thackeray, whom we had met on the boat coming from Wilmington, fell a victim to their wiles. After taking a ride out of Charleston, he came back to find that he had been *dévalisé*. His luggage ransacked and his money gone, he appealed to Thackeray, his kinsman, who, with wonted liberality, allowed his young friend to get back to his regiment at the end of his furlough.   As a sequel he and his brother gave me a banquet in Paris at the Maison Dorée, as he was passing through on his way to the Crimea. The dinner was sumptuous, but on examining the *menu* the critical garçon exclaimed, horrified : *"Pas de rôti, monsieur?"* as if the absence of the *pièce de résistance* was a breach of the known laws of gastronomy.   This exclamation increased our joviality. This note must be closed with a sad appendix as to

SHOPPING, CHARLESTON, VA.

A GROUP OF MARKET-WOMEN

the fate of this promising officer. He was one of the gallant band told off to explode the docks of Sebastopol. There seemed to be a hitch and a delay in the firing of the mine; he rushed to examine the cause, and it immediately burst up, killing him on the spot. He was the last victim of this lengthy siege and of the operations in the Crimea, I believe.

Leaving Charleston and its gallant host of convivial friendships, we went thence to Savannah in Georgia, the furthest goal of our journey. We reached it in a small steamer—of low draught, owing to the numerous shallows in the red-coloured river leading to this capital. We now arrived in a land unpaved and without kerbstones to the gangways, which were mere sand-tracks. These had the great advantage of being noiseless. We were driven to a primitive hotel, the home, as we soon discovered, of legions of fleas and other questionable gentry. Those who had the "White Squall" ballad by heart were reminded of the passage

"Then all the fleas in Jewry
Jumped up and bit like fury;"

or of that *Punch* cartoon of an "Arabian Night's Entertainment." The next morning, on coming into the chief's bed-room, I noticed the floor and chairs strewn with lucifers, ignited during the night to try and catch these disturbers of peace. His face and limbs were blotched and bumped with the horrid marks of the fray; but balm and salve appeared in the form of our cheery and hospitable English Consul, Mr. Low, who insisted on harbouring first Thackeray

AT THE "CLARENDON"

and then myself in his delightful private residence, during our stay here. There was one never-failing barometer of contentment noticeable in Titmarshian avocations, which was whenever he took up his gold nib for illustration of whatever struck his fancy at the time. At Mr. Low's quarters many such were produced. One of these, for instance, has been reproduced in fac-simile in Miss Adelaide Procter's pleasant publication the " *Victoria Regia* " for 1861. It is a capital sketch of a little negro servant, for whom the descriptive text invents the apt word of " Black-a-moorkin," not as yet adopted into the latest dictionaries of the English language. I am unaware whether this sketch was done on the occasion of his first visit, or on the second lecturing tour, as no date is affixed to it. But whether this is so or not, I give, as it were, a faint pictorial echo of mine of the same subject, as it includes the interesting figure of a Chinese divinity student, upon whose pigtail the pickaninny had looked with undisguised wonderment as he presented him with a cup of coffee. He used to give a backward scrape of his bare foot, by way of acknowledgment, when a coin came out of the Thackerayan open purse.

The endeavours to sketch the juvenile negroes in the streets I found almost impossible, owing to their extra restlessness of limb and feature, as the mere

11

fact of staring at them set them off into laughter-
convulsions.

In the afternoon, at school-closing time, we met

THE CHINESE DIVINITY STUDENT

the gleeful groups of boys, both black and white,
escaping from their class-rooms. Accosting one of
the small negro-boys, Thackeray asked him, with
a view less of testing his knowledge than of

Broadway, April 6th '53.
F.V.C.

BROADWAY FASHIONS

benevolent purpose, to spell Con-stan-ti-no-ple. This proving beyond him, he missed his tip, and went off tumbling head over heels in the sand-tracked street.

More steady were the old hands, some of whom ministered to the juvenile cravings for pea-nuts and for ground-cake. Here (p. 165) is one of them I noticed sitting on the corner of Calhoun Street, as she chats with an old crony asking after her health. Her answer, I recollect, was, "Thank you, I'm mending smart."

Fires flare here, even more fiercely than in other towns of the States, the buildings being mostly constructed of wood. Thirty years before this time whole

BONAVENTURA, NEAR SAVANNAH

sections had been swept away, yet a few buildings that were spared have the picturesque construction of old plaster-and-beam architecture.

The quays were piled with cotton-bales, testifying to the industry of the negro - hands ; and to the staple production of the district, which was whisked about on trollies, the charioteer standing bolt upright on his booted legs, holding the reins.

South. Carolina

PEA-NUTS

The town outskirts afford pleasant walks.

Four miles from Savannah is one of the sights to which everyone trends. It is called Bonaventura, which seems somewhat of a misnomer. That Tuscan patron-saint wrote a book with the title of "Lignum Vitæ," *i.e.*, the Cross, which he decks miraculously with foliage. Here, by an odd freak of arboriculture, the tree's foliage is covered over by

a drooping funereal lichen resembling a perpetual
downpour of rain; well suited, however, to the destination of the cemetery, which it shelters with its
lachrymose fronds. The trees are live oaks, with
a parasitical growth which I have not noticed elsewhere. I tried to catch its effect in appropriate
water-colour.

Towards the end of March the lecturing was over.
We bade farewell to the kindest of hosts, Mr. Low,
our Consul at Savannah. Though the mosquito as yet
did not worry, the weather began to be unpleasantly
hot.

We returned to Charleston, which was also getting

A NEW YORK CONGREGATION

a dash of summer sun at this early time. Our eyes, freshened by green Georgian pastures, now felt the effects of too prolonged contemplation of brick-and-mortar frontages. If you happen to be yourself sleepless at night, the snoring slumbers heard through thin partitions seem to aggravate your restlessness. We therefore left hospitable Charleston, and returned once more to our comfortable quarters at the "Clarendon Hotel," New York. Not without disquiet Thackeray heard there of the precarious health of some of the elder members of his family in Europe.

When we returned to New York, making a final stay there of about a fortnight, it was partly with the intention of going to Canada as a lecturing *finale;* but by repetition the task had grown wearisome, as before hinted. This and other reasons finally prevailing against further venture, the notion was abandoned. This two weeks' interval was pleasantly filled up. I made a few sketches for the Appleton firm, who paid me liberally. I also painted a portrait of Mr. Henry James, the father of the renowned novelist-playwright, now amongst us, which was pronounced very like; and I did this *con amore*, not only with a view to please Mrs. James, to whom it was presented, but being personally delighted to limn the features of one who had proved himself so doughty a champion and admirer of Thackeray in the press of that day.

CHAPTER V

FROM New York a pleasant diversion suggested itself at this time. On Monday, April 11th, we took the train from New York to Albany, giving us a pleasant glimpse of woodland and river scenery all the way. On our arrival we were met by a jovial skipper-friend of Thackeray's. His great anxiety was to sequestrate the lecturer in the privacy of his hotel, with the idea of only giving the privilege of seeing him to those willing to pay for it at the lecture-hall. This had naturally the contrary effect to that intended, as Thackeray was at once seized with an intense desire to walk about and to see the town for himself; so we sallied out with that view. The visit was well timed, as the jaded members of the twin houses—the Senate and the Representatives—had only two or three session-days left before disbanding, their salaries being only payable for 200 sittings, which then expired, when relaxation of duty coincided naturally with stoppage of salary. The then Capitol was a plain brown-stone building, since this period replaced by a granite structure of far greater pretentions architecturally. So I suppose the cosy homely abode of the Senate, as I then sketched it, with its circular benches groaning under piles of

THE SENATE, ALBANY

reports and reference volumes—its members chatting together in nooks and corners, whilst the orator, scarcely listened to, was holding forth, and its president sitting on an elevated bench under the portrait of General Washington—have all disappeared, and have made way for more imposing senatorial decorum. The town itself had at this time but few vestiges of the old Dutch style of architecture, or even of the bricks, which themselves used to be in the olden time imported here from Holland.

On the 12th the second lecture was given, and I think, immediately after it was over, we got into the Hudson River steamer, which brought us back to New York. The papers had announced that Montreal would next be visited, but Thackeray had possibly already changed his mind on the subject of further deliveries of the lectures; and this turned out to be the last given in the United States—a welcome windup to him.

Thackeray's pen was not idle. He wrote at this comfortable New York hostelry the now famous sonnet, "Lucy's Birthday," which is dated 15th April. Within a month of writing this, I had the pleasure, at the friendly intercession of the author's daughter, Mrs. Ritchie, of meeting this lady, who came over to this country for the first time. Her presence reminded me of the ever-charming welcome I received in the midst of that New York household, that of Mr. and Mrs. Baxter.

At this time the absorbing topic was a Washington telegram, startling political quidnuncs. It was to the effect that President Pierce had given the appointment of the Madrid Embassy to Mr. Pierre

Soulé. When it was first flashed over the wires, people fond of making diplomatic forecasts prognosticated that this meant the proximate purchase of the island of Cuba from Spain. This solution of a long-pending difficulty was amended so as to suggest the acquisition of this possession, leaving out financial considerations; an arrangement which subsequent events, as every-body knows, completely falsified. However, this shrewd-looking, bright - eyed senator became the hero of the hour, and as such his semblance at this time is here introduced. The ardent, though good-humoured, advocates for and against annexation used to meet in places, and you over-heard them discussing the topic good-humouredly thus over the fragrant produce of the island itself, and doubtless they made the best of what portion of Havannah could be got.

The signal for departure took place with the suddenness of a thunder-clap. I visited Thackeray in his room in the early morning. He had a newspaper in his hand, and he said, " I see there's a Cunarder going this morning," which happened to be the 20th of

April. " I'll go down to Wall Street to see whether I can secure berths in her; meanwhile, try and see all the traps packed up and ready." As we were

old campaigners, the thing was done and the bills paid in the nick of time. The only people we had time to shake hands with were the friendly family of the Baxters. One of the ladies, I regret to say, wrote wittily afterwards to this effect, " We shall never forgive Mr. Crowe for the cheerful expression upon his face the day he went away ! "

Who does not sigh for home at the end of six months, wherever that domicile may be ? At about eleven o'clock we were speeding down Broadway ; we got into a boat on the East River, and were greeted by the shipping agent's shout, " Hurry up — she's starting ! " and we had hardly had time to get on board when we were going full steam on to Sandy Hook. The name of the ship was the *Europa;* the winds were propitious, and at times all sail was set.

One of the officers, I remember, told us he was on board the vessel Dickens went out in. Thackeray asked him whether, in a sailor's estimation, the passage had been as terrific as was recorded in the famous "Notes," when he corroborated the Dickensian version in every particular. Our ship had fair weather.

Regardless of another injustice to old Ireland, and although not many miles from inland Skibbereen, when we noticed the picturesquely perched lighthouse on the rock of Cape Clear we shouted out "Old England!" in the bright, early morning air.

We coasted the green-clad cliffs of Cork, and next morning, Sunday, we stepped once more upon the Liverpool landing stage, and got housed again in the "Adelphi" there. An interval of six months, almost to a day and to an hour, had elapsed since our departure on our first passage across the Atlantic.

The six months' sojourn in the United States, the two passages across the Atlantic inclusive, were sandwiched, as it were, between the two great efforts of the Thackerayan pen, "Esmond," and "The Newcomes." Family ties, balmy rest for the body from overstrained travel, and search after the inspiriting literary tonic ever given him by a Parisian visit, led

Thackeray to his favourite Champs Élysées once more; and my modest avocation as pen-holder being at an end, I also came to the same city in search of artistic relaxation. In the month of October, 1853, came out the first number of "The Newcomes," which was illustrated by the facile and graceful pencil of Richard Doyle. The second number, that of November, came to hand in Paris in its yellow cover complete. The author, who had not before seen the illustrations to the text, was much put out on seeing one of these, in which the games of the Charterhouse boys were grouped. There were football, leap-frog, and wrestling going on in mid-distance. The foreground is admirably composed with the scene of the youngster drawing upon his banker, Clive, for his needed coin. The peccant accessory which roused the wrath of the writer was the group of two boys playing at marbles on the left of the spectator. "Why," said the irate author, "they would as soon have thought of cutting off their heads as play at marbles at the Charterhouse." This woodcut was, I noticed, suppressed altogether in subsequent editions. Nor was this a solitary instance of tardy regret on the author's part. As much of the subordinate interest of the novel lay in its keen insight into art-life and manners, he asked me to introduce him to my friend Gérôme, the world-renowned painter of so many *chefs-d'œuvre*. I brought

him one day to see the cluster of friendly studios, of
which Gérôme's was the central one, in the Rue Notre-
Dame-des-Champs—a quarter haunted by the spirit of
Ste.-Beuve and other *literati* in former days. We
found the painter had just completed his large
composition entitled the "Apotheosis of Augustus,"
now honourably placed in the Amiens Museum.
Opposite to it on the walls of his studio was a
beautifully-finished but small composition, which
Thackeray whispered to me he should like to become
possessor of; but he weighed this in his mind, and
said nothing to the author of it. The studios of Brion,
the Alsatian painter, who gave you in art the same
delicate pictures of life strewed in the pages of Erck-
mann and Chatrian; Schützenberger, a clever draughts-
man of scenes from the same locality; Toulmouche,
the skilful illustrator of manners and modes of the last
century and of our own time, one and all threw open
their doors to welcome him. His exclamation, after
our leave-taking was over, and when we strolled back
through the picturesque avenues of the Luxembourg
Gardens, was, "I wish I had seen this before!"

It is mere conjecture on my part; but the impression left upon me at the time was that the "grand
serenity" to which he alluded, pervading this mental
atmosphere, if previously received as an impression,
might have helped to modify his artistic lucubrations

in "The Newcomes." The efforts of Clive Newcome, and those of J. J., earnest as the latter are, seldom escape the bonds of amateurishness. The great romance, on the other hand, might have suffered by deviating from its intended course. The incident is here noted as indicative of the waves of indecision, assailing at times fixed literary resolves. No one, now, is there, who would not regret that one sentence of that romance were either altered or scored off.

I now once more got into pictorial harness; and, to my delight, I found Thackeray's kindly prediction "that I should be none the worse for the short break in my artistic career" fully verified.

Cape · Clear.

INDEX

For EU product safety concerns, contact us at Calle de José Abascal, 56–1°, 28003 Madrid, Spain or eugpsr@cambridge.org.

www.ingramcontent.com/pod-product-compliance
Ingram Content Group UK Ltd.
Pitfield, Milton Keynes, MK11 3LW, UK
UKHW012345130625
459647UK00009B/550